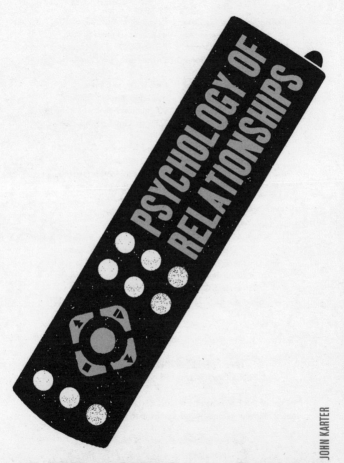

PSYCHOLOGY OF RELATIONSHIPS

JOHN KARTER

A PRACTICAL GUIDE

38 0673 1

D0529909

Published in the UK in 2012
by Icon Books Ltd,
Omnibus Business Centre,
39–41 North Road,
London N7 9DP
email: info@iconbooks.co.uk
www.iconbooks.co.uk

Sold in the UK, Europe,
South Africa and Asia
by Faber & Faber Ltd,
Bloomsbury House,
74–77 Great Russell Street,
London WC1B 3DA
or their agents

Distributed in the UK, Europe,
South Africa and Asia
by TBS Ltd,
TBS Distribution Centre,
Colchester Road,
Frating Green,
Colchester CO7 7DW

Published in Australia in 2012
by Allen & Unwin Pty Ltd,
PO Box 8500, 83 Alexander Street,
Crows Nest, NSW 2065

Distributed in Canada
by Penguin Books Canada,
90 Eglinton Avenue East, Suite 700,
Toronto, Ontario M4P 2Y3

Published in the USA in 2012
by Totem Books
Inquiries to: Icon Books Ltd,
Omnibus Business Centre,
39–41 North Road,
London N7 9DP, UK

Distributed to the trade in the USA
by Consortium Book Sales
and Distribution
The Keg House, 34 Thirteenth
Avenue NE, Suite 101,
Minneapolis, MN 55413-1007

ISBN: 978-184831-359-0

Typeset in Avenir by Marie Doherty

Printed and bound in the UK by Clays Ltd, St Ives plc

About the author

John Karter is a UKCP registered psychotherapist in private practice. He has worked as a therapist in various settings, including GamCare, the national association for gambling care; a child, adolescent and family unit of the NHS; and secondary and further education. He has been a tutor in psychotherapy and counselling at Regent's College School of Psychotherapy and Counselling Psychology and Richmond upon Thames College. He is the author of *On Training To Be A Therapist* (Open University Press), which is used as a standard textbook on training courses. John has been a writer for *The Sunday Times*, *The Times* and *The Independent*, and is also the author of a novella entitled *The Profit* (Roastbooks).

Acknowledgements

Sincere thanks to Susi Noble and Katerina Dimakopoulou for reading through the manuscript and making invaluable comments and suggestions. I am also grateful to Duncan Heath, Harry Scoble and everyone else at Icon Books for their professionalism and support in bringing this book from basic manuscript to finished article.

Author's note

It's important to note that there is much frequently-used research employed in the psychology of relationships.

Where I know the source I have been sure to reference it, but my apologies here to the originators of any material if I have overlooked them.

Contents

About the author   iii
Acknowledgements   v
Author's note   vi

Introduction   1

1: Knowing your needs   7
2: A game of two halves   19
3: All by myself   31
4: Growing together, apart   43
5: All change, please   55
6: Are you receiving me?   67
7: The self-esteem factor   81
8: The meaning of conflict   95
9: Crazy for you   109
10: The parent trap   121
11: Why opposites rarely attract   135
12: Knowing me, knowing you   147
13: The myth of sex   159
14: Forsaking all others?   171
15: The mystery of love   183

Conclusions   197

Resources   201
Index   207

Introduction

Grow old with me! The best is yet to be.
Robert Browning

This is not another book about love or how to find love; there are more than enough of those out there already. My aim is to help you to understand your relationships and to achieve new and healthier ways of relating by explaining some of the major underlying psychological principles and 'drivers' that lead us to think and behave in certain ways with our spouses or partners. Identifying and working on these motivating factors will help to eliminate 'knee-jerk' reactions and will nourish and sustain the relationship instead of allowing it to plod along and deteriorate by default.

Working as a psychotherapist, I encounter the full range of psychological drama and complexity through the stories clients tell me about their lives. Yet, no matter how often I peer into the kaleidoscope of passion, joy, sorrow, and the whole range of emotions that constitute what it means to be human, I am still surprised by the widespread misconceptions that people hold about major life issues.

High on the list of these beliefs are the expectations people have of their relationships. For the purposes of this book I am referring to love/romantic relationships between adults, both heterosexual and same-sex; although some of the principles in this book can be applied to relationships generally.

Most readers will, I'm sure, be familiar with the adage 'Who ever said life was meant to be easy?' which, despite its intrinsic flippancy, contains a fundamental truth. For many, there is an assumption that success and happiness should be handed to us on a silver platter; that those states of being are, if you like, an inherent and inalienable part of our birthright. In the case of relationships, there is often an expectation that these 'love partnerships' should not only provide a permanent state of bliss but alleviate all the difficulties of living as well.

It's natural and healthy to dream of finding someone with whom we can enjoy a joyful, nurturing, fulfilling relationship. However, when we buy into the widespread idea that harmony and mutual fulfilment happen automatically as a result of meeting the 'right' person, an important factor is missed, or dismissed. Meaningful, lasting relationships are incredibly complex, multi-faceted psychological structures that are not built in a day and do not happen purely by accident.

That is certainly not intended to offer a negative take on what can be the most sublime and uplifting of all human experiences; rather it flags up a key principle of this book, namely that the more you put into relationships, both in terms of effort and understanding, the more you get out of them.

Like so many things in life, the index of success in relationships almost invariably correlates with the amount of sustained attention, effort and, occasionally, self-sacrifice that each partner is prepared to bring to it. In this context, I am reminded of Gary Player's response when asked for the secret of his phenomenal success as a champion golfer: 'The harder I practise the luckier I get.' Other qualities such as caring, nurturing, giving, and, of course, genuine loving, play a huge part as well but these do not preclude the need for working at a relationship to ensure its continued stability and growth.

A relationship that is taken for granted, not worked at to some degree, or where either partner (or both) does not respect the other as a person, downplays or dismisses their needs, makes no attempt at meaningful communication, and does not honour certain boundaries of behaviour, will almost invariably wither and eventually die.

This is where the psychological basis of a relationship kicks in, which means, paradoxically, that working at it is often not enough in itself. Given those complicated and often delicate underpinnings – which are usually out of our awareness or in our 'unconscious', to use the psychological term – focusing on the 'visible' issues, such as better communication, acceptance of the other person's human failings, and learning to deal with change, needs to be supplemented by an understanding of what is really going on beneath the surface of the dialogue and interactions.

The more you are able to gain insight into the hidden agendas, feelings and unspoken communications, and uncover what is really happening between the two of you, the better placed you will be to deal with conflict, change negative and destructive patterns of relating that eat away at the fabric of the relationship, and bring those vital qualities of mutual nurture, respect and genuine love into play.

When couples are suddenly able to see what lies beneath their 'locked-in' behaviour patterns it can mark a turning point in their relationship. And often it is something relatively simple in psychological terms that goes unrecognized, simply because the individuals concerned have not been made aware of it. That was the case with Bill and Angie, who came to see me because they were caught up in a seemingly endless cycle of arguing and recrimination, which had descended to the level of increasingly bitter personal attacks.

After listening to them both putting their own side of the story, I asked them if my perception that neither was prepared to back down in any way was true. Rather sheepishly, they agreed that was the case. When I suggested to them that pride was the basis for their stubborn refusal to give ground, and explained that this was linked to a perceived loss of self-esteem, or loss of face, it was as if a veil had been lifted from their eyes.

In the next session they told me that things had already taken a turn for the better because every time an argument began to kick in they had been able to step back and acknowledge their own feelings of vulnerability, and, most importantly, listen to what the other was trying to communicate instead of hitting back. Relationship issues do not usually resolve themselves quite so easily, but in this case a simple insight had sparked a sea change in their way of relating to each other.

If you are struggling to understand why your dreams of emotional harmony and sexual ecstasy are crumbling before your eyes; why he or she is proving to be anything but the model of loving kindness you expected them to be; or why you have descended into a living hell of rowing and resentment, my hope is that the following chapters will help you find a way to step back, see things from a new perspective and begin to move forward in a more positive direction, as in the example of Bill and Angie above.

On the other hand, perhaps you are simply seeking to gain more insight into your relationship, to see how it functions on different levels, and make it more loving and rewarding than it already is. Or maybe you are keen to understand relationships in general and so be better equipped for entering into one when you are ready. In either case the principles and practical pointers in this book are also designed to put you on a sound footing for achieving those goals.

The celebrated American author James Thurber once said: 'A lady of 47 who has been married 27 years and has six children knows what love really is and once described it for me like this: "Love is what you've been through with somebody."'

It is my hope that the following pages will make the 'going through' a more joyful, more fulfilling experience.

John Karter

1. Knowing your needs

*One of the oldest human needs is having someone
to wonder where you are when you don't come home
at night.*
Margaret Mead

We can't choose our parents but we can choose our partners, to paraphrase the well-known saying. However, when we enter into a relationship with someone, the 'choosing' is not as straightforward as it seems on a surface level, because it is usually underpinned by a multi-layered mix of emotional, psychological and biological factors going on behind the scenes.

Leaving aside those hidden agendas for the moment, the primary motivation for seeking a relationship is to fulfil a need, or in most cases a combination of needs. The list of relationship needs is as long as it is diverse, and the level and scope of an individual's needs is as unique as a fingerprint.

Here, in no particular order, are some of the principal needs that drive relationships (the list is by no means exhaustive):

Giving and receiving love/affection/intimacy
Curing loneliness

Companionship
Security
Having children
Sexual fulfilment
Complying with pressure from society/parents/media
Validation of self
Power and control
Personal growth

- Make a list of the needs you had when you entered into your current or most recent relationship. Try to be as honest as you can with yourself.
- How many of those needs have been met either in full or in part?
- How many of them have not been met at all?
- During the course of the relationship, have you recognized new needs and/or discarded some of the original ones?
- What do you think your partner's needs were/are? Do you think he/she feels those needs have been met?

If your answers to the above surprise you, remember that most of us enter into a relationship spontaneously, without considering why we are really doing it, and, more importantly, what we need from it. People are either driven by nature and instinct, for example the fundamental biological need to reproduce, or are led by their heart rather than their head.

Taking the heart route is human and exciting, but it does leave us open to the very real possibility of falling into something that is more about what we want than what we need. Most of us are so focused on what we *expect* to get, based on romantic ideals, cultural norms and media propaganda, that the qualities, standards, values and emotional input we actually need to be happy and fulfilled within a relationship are ignored.

Emerging from the honeymoon phase

During the honeymoon phase, by which I mean not the week or two-week long getaway following the wedding, but the early stages of a relationship when everything is new and exciting, both partners' needs can happily lie dormant. The experience of being together in the bubble of exclusivity they have created around themselves is enough.

However, that high inevitably begins to wane as reality sets in. The individuals concerned begin to emerge from what feels like a period of complete mental and physical merging, or 'the Velcro phase', as the comedian Lenny Henry memorably described it. When that happens, couples begin to become aware of their individual needs, and this will begin to impact the relationship in a positive or negative way, depending on how it is handled.

Dealing with the day-to-day business of being with someone, who, in some respects, you may not know in any real depth, is when the real test of that relationship begins. I would say that in almost all cases people bring needs into their relationships that have not been communicated to the other person. This in turn conjures up unspoken expectations of their partner, and assumptions about the relationship itself and how it is going to be, a situation that provides an instant recipe for conflict.

To complicate matters, many of these needs are unconscious and have therefore not been recognized or thought about by the one who has them. Some of these unconscious needs may relate to unresolved childhood matters, such as 'unfinished business' with a parent, or emotional wounds sustained during an individual's early years, which they carry into adult relationships.

Neglectful approach to a life-changing event

For example, a fairly common scenario would be for one partner to enter into a relationship with a need for stability, security and having children, but contained within those primary needs there might be subsidiary or unconscious needs. These could relate to issues such as low self-esteem and shame, which originated in childhood. In many cases these needs are not talked about in any meaningful way, or not even mentioned at all, which, compared to the way we proceed in other areas of our lives, is an extraordinarily neglectful approach to a major event that is life-changing and significant on many levels.

If you want to buy a car, computer or television set, you make a list of the features you want that car, computer or TV to have; then you communicate those features to the salesperson. If you went into a store and said 'I'd like a computer, please', and left it at that, not only would you almost certainly end up with an item that lacked many of the essentials you desired, you would also get a very strange look from the salesperson! Yet that kind of casual, non-specific attitude is exactly how we regularly embark on relationships.

Unconscious needs are a different matter because these are out of awareness and until they have been consciously acknowledged they cannot be talked about or dealt with. And, as we shall see in the following chapter, if an individual seeks out a partner to 'fix' them – that is to say, in order to compensate for the emotional difficulties that he or she is experiencing – that is not a healthy way of relating.

Jenny

Jenny presented a classic example of unspoken, unmet needs. She came to see me suffering from a low-level 'background' depression which allowed her to function on a day-to-day level but robbed her of any hope of real happiness and fulfilment. She did not know why she felt that way or how she could begin to change things around. It transpired that Jenny was the classic 'doormat', submitting herself totally to her husband's needs, which included having sex every night without exception, and keeping the house spotless and the children quiet at all times.

Her own needs for affection, respect and validation as a worthwhile human being, wife and mother were totally dismissed by her husband. She went along with this unhappy situation partly because she was scared of him, but also because no one had told her that needs are like seeds – they need to be nurtured or they will wither and die. And that, as Jenny realized when I pointed it out to her, is a major cause of depression and lack of fulfilment, as well as relationship breakdown.

Sadly, Jenny had an ingrained belief that her life was destined to be like that, based on her experiences of being emotionally neglected and abused by her father (and, to a certain extent, her mother) as a child. Her 'life script' told her that her needs were unimportant compared to those of her family, and that any attempt to get those personal needs met was being self-indulgent and uncaring, a view that was reinforced by her husband's bullying, selfish behaviour towards her.

Because of this, my work with Jenny focused on helping her to gain insight into the way she 'set up' situations to maintain her life script. Eventually she was able to see that she had unconsciously chosen her husband because he reminded her of her uncaring, abusive father. This was a classic example of 'transference' (a concept dealt with in more detail later in this book), whereby an experience from the past is 'transferred' to the present.

The ideal of love

There is not sufficient space in this book to go through the various relationship needs in detail, although many of them will be touched on in some form in other chapters. Research shows that love, security and having children, regularly top the charts, with love being offered as the number one response to most questionnaires on the subject.

Love, which is the subject of the final chapter, is a very human and laudable need to have and to pursue in a relationship, but how often do we stop and think what we really mean when we use the word 'love'? In other words, what need or needs lie beneath this emotive four-letter word used so freely in adult interactions? Rather than delving into that question, many people carry around a vague, romantic ideal of love as portrayed by Keats:

> *I have been astonished that men could die martyrs for*
> *their religion –*
> *I have shudder'd at it.*
> *I shudder no more.*
> *I could be martyr'd for my religion*
> *Love is my religion*
> *And I could die for that.*
> *I could die for you.*

In the final analysis, love is just a word and it can mean many different things to different people. Words are essentially symbolic; they are, if you like, verbal signposts to the actions, things, thoughts and emotions they stand for. So, in the majority of cases, 'love' is the surface need and might represent only one element of a person's overall needs, or might not be the real need at all.

When we talk of needing 'love', we might mean understanding, companionship, intimacy, sex, validation, or a combination of those and other needs as well. That is why it is so vital to try to uncover what lies beneath the surface by making yourself aware of your own areas of need (as in the exercise on page 8), including your aspirations, dreams, psychological problem areas, and also the values and standards that are important to you.

By doing this you will play your part in placing the relationship on a healthy footing from the start. It is almost a truism to say that if your needs are met you will be happier and more fulfilled and therefore more able to cater for your partner's needs. A word of caution, though: sometimes we give to our partners what *we* need in the mistaken belief that this is what *they* need too.

Beware of gender myths

Much has been written about the differing needs of men and women, and it is undoubtedly true that, to a certain extent, gender dictates what we need to make us happy in a relationship. In particular, it is fair to say that men and women are 'wired' differently in terms of emotional responses. It can also be said that men tend to build their sense of self primarily around their careers and achievements; whereas women do this more through their relationships with partners and family. However, with the traditional roles of the sexes being blurred more and more, this is no longer as valid as it might once have been.

In my opinion, too much has been made of the apparently unbridgeable gulf between the sexes, to a point where men and women are portrayed as verging on different species. This is exemplified in the bestselling book, *Men are from Mars, Women are from Venus*, where the author lists the different 'primary love needs' of men and women as follows:

Women: caring, understanding, respect, devotion, validation, reassurance

Men: trust, acceptance, appreciation, admiration, approval, encouragement.

I would say that all these needs are interchangeable: to a greater or lesser degree, women need the qualities on the men's list and vice-versa. People's needs are based on their individual emotional make-up and personality and are not simply products of their gender, even though gender does have some influence.

Going along with these 'great divides' simply prolongs stereotyping that brings about self-fulfilling prophecies; in other words people behave in ways they are traditionally expected to behave according to the gender myths. So when Hollywood actress Sharon Stone says: 'Women might be able to fake orgasms, but men can fake a whole relationship' it might be perceived as humorous, but it simply reinforces those tired old stereotypes and does nothing to help women – or men – understand their partners; quite the opposite in fact.

The effect of time

Another key factor to be aware of in understanding relationship needs is that they invariably change over time. So, for example, the need for sex can diminish as we age – though not necessarily and not as completely as some people would have us believe! Sexual needs can be replaced or complemented by the need for affection and companionship. Similarly, the need for security and validation can also diminish if we begin to feel more fulfilled and confident in ourselves and/or within our relationship.

But perhaps the most important thing to acknowledge when contemplating your own needs is your absolute right to have them, and to have them met to at least a reasonable extent. Human needs, especially psychological and emotional ones, have all too frequently received a bad press; there is a widespread misconception that they are a sign of being weak, psychologically flawed or overly demanding, so we hear of people being talked of in a derogatory way as 'needy'.

If your partner is constantly demanding attention and nothing you do appears to satisfy their demands, this is cause for concern and might well indicate a deep-seated psychological issue that would benefit from professional help, such as counselling. However, adopting a stance where one's own needs are all that matter, to the detriment or dismissal of your partner's, is vastly different to simply seeking to receive what you need in fundamental terms in order to be happy within a relationship.

So, when another Hollywood actress, Audrey Hepburn, said: 'I was born with an enormous need for affection, and a terrible need to give it' there are two ways of looking at her apparent self-criticism. If her need to receive and give affection was all–consuming and 'blind' it would clearly impact negatively on any relationship.

However, if Hepburn was merely highlighting the fact that mutual affection was an important, non-negotiable element of a relationship for her, then that was simply being human as well as practical. When we examine the factors that make for a healthy and viable relationship, understanding the difference between those two states of mind is paramount.

In the next chapter we will examine a major need that has not been mentioned so far, one that is often seen as the principal motivation for a relationship, namely seeking someone who will 'complete' us.

- Make a conscious effort to recognize your needs and communicate them to your partner early on in the relationship.

- Be realistic in your expectations; no one can fulfil their partner's needs completely and continually.

- People's needs vary, so try to allow for the fact that you and your partner's needs will be different.

- Remember that discussion and compromise are the key when one partner feels their needs are not being met.

Needs are human and crucially important; if they remain unspoken and unmet they can become one of the most corrosive aspects of a relationship.

2. A game of two halves

I complete me. I just got lucky that, after I completed myself, I met someone who could tolerate me.
Sandra Bullock

Most people entering a relationship hope that it will provide an environment of love, security and validation – a space where they can feel respected and special, and so build a platform from which to face the world and grow as a person. That is certainly not an unreasonable aspiration to have, provided it is seen as a mutual undertaking in which the two people concerned are both responsible for creating the state of nurture and happiness.

The word 'mutual' cannot be stressed enough, because one of the fundamental mistakes people make is to think that they have to do very little or nothing at all; that finding the right relationship will provide the answer to all their problems and make them happy and fulfilled in itself. Implicit within that belief is the conviction that their partner is capable of bringing this about simply by being who they are.

To recycle the familiar football cliché, they see it as a game of two halves in which two people who are a perfect 'fit' come together and provide each other with the 'missing part' of themselves. This in turn creates an overriding need to find the 'other half' who will bring about the completion of the 'divided' self.

Ancient roots of the 'other half' myth

The 'other-half' need has widespread and ancient roots that can be traced back as far as ancient Greece in the 3rd and 4th centuries BCE. In a speech by the playwright Aristophanes in Plato's *Symposium* we read that the first humans were androgynous creatures with four hands and four feet, a single head with two faces on a single neck, and two sets of genitals.

These unified humans were extremely powerful and dared to challenge the gods. However, the gods feared that if they killed off the humans they would have no one to worship them, so Zeus decreed that all humans should be cut in half so their power would be diminished.

This physical splitting meant that humans became engaged in an interminable search for their other halves and on finding each other they were 'lost in an amazement of love and friendship and intimacy'. The story has echoes in a well-known Biblical text, specifically Genesis, chapter 2, where, after God has created humans he says: 'It is not good for the man to be alone'. Later on in the chapter we read: 'For this reason a man will leave his father and mother and be united to his wife, and they will become one flesh.'

The term 'soul mate' stems from this idea of completion by another human being. The concept has become so widely accepted that it is part of the language of love and is frequently used by dating agencies when they advertise their services. In *Love By Numbers*, Dr Luisa Dillner highlights a Gallup survey of 1000 Americans in their twenties showing that almost 90 per cent of them believed there is a soul mate 'waiting for you somewhere out there'.

When people mention the idea of a soul mate they talk of such things as agreeing on major life issues, sharing the same background and passions, and having an instinctive ability to understand you, and even to know what you are thinking before you have said it. Hence people who believe they have found their soul mate say things like: 'It was almost as if he could read my mind', 'It was as if we had known each other for years', or 'It was amazing the way we completed each other's sentences'.

- Consider whether you genuinely believe everyone has a soul mate or 'other half' who can complete them as a person.

- Whether you have found your soul mate or not, ask yourself what expectations you have or would have of such a person.

- If you are with someone you believed to be your soul mate when you met them, how far have they gone towards fulfilling those expectations?

- Take some time and consider whether your expectations were realistic or based purely on getting your own needs met.

It is true that having a caring partner who respects and admires you and makes you feel special can work wonders for self-esteem and emotional well-being in general. It is wonderful when you meet someone who appears to offer the immediate understanding and empathy all human beings crave and deserve. However, the concept of finding our other half is fraught with hidden dangers.

The first is the unrealistic belief that we have found some kind of super-being, who is free of the usual human faults and frailties. If such a person exists they must hail from another planet because they are certainly not from this one. Second, and far more insidious in terms of fulfilling needs and expectations, is the idea that this person has the ability to heal us in emotional terms, to make us completely happy and fulfilled, and, above all, to complete us.

Only you can heal yourself

As the quotation from Sandra Bullock at the start of this chapter makes clear, the only person who can complete you is yourself. Nobody else, no matter how loving, understanding or caring they are, can fill the emotional void inside you, which is what many people assume finding their other half, or soul mate, is about. In essence, this amounts to a 'Fix me!' demand to your partner, and has echoes of the situation in which people go to see psychotherapists and counsellors expecting to be given a magical solution to their problems.

A good therapist will offer the kind of understanding, empathy and gentle nudging that enables their clients to find the resources to deal with their own problems; being a helpful guide as they climb the mountain, if you like. But in terms of getting out there and doing it, the client has to 'walk the talk' himself. Similarly, in relationships, a caring partner can be there for you and can empathize with you and support you, but he or she cannot live your life for you and certainly cannot be expected to 'magic away' any emotional difficulties you might have.

In this context, one of the phenomena that never ceases to amaze me in my work as a psychotherapist is the number of intelligent, insightful people who expect their partners to be paragons of love, support and nurture at all times, no matter what they are going through themselves; to feel affectionate and in the mood for sex whatever the circumstances, and also to have the gift of mind-reading.

When their partner falls below these expectations, which of course they often do, it is seen as the partner's fault rather than as a sign that they should examine their own deep-seated emotional needs and issues and try to work on whatever it is that is making them feel so unhappy with themselves and the relationship. Blaming your partner for failing to 'fix' you is a common cause of conflict, and can only be resolved if the person doing the blaming is prepared to take a long, hard look at themselves and admit that it is *their* problem.

The search for 'missing parts'

The search for a person who can complete us means we are often attracted to people who possess qualities we lack ourselves (conversely we can be irritated when partners exhibit characteristics or behaviour we find annoying in ourselves). So, for example, if someone lacks confidence and self-esteem, they might be drawn to a partner who appears confident and happy in his or her own skin, or even someone who is arrogant and conceited.

Similarly, someone who is scared of taking risks might be attracted to an individual who is prepared to throw caution to the wind in their business or social life, quite possibly even a gambler who offers a glimpse of the kind of excitement the other partner feels is missing from their own life. In so doing, the cautious partner can get in touch with that lost or disowned part of themselves and live a more adventurous life through their partner (this is sometimes known as living 'vicariously').

In this respect, the old saying 'opposites attract' is true, although it is important to be aware that finding someone who thinks and acts in ways that are totally unlike your own is certainly not a recipe for instant bliss; quite the opposite in many cases because the qualities that were initially perceived as desirable in the other person can eventually prove to be irritating or even unbearable (Chapter 11 is devoted to the question of whether opposites attract).

The celebrated psychologist Carl Jung highlighted one major source of this 'missing part' attraction. He coined the terms 'anima', to denote the unconscious feminine component of men, and 'animus', to denote the unconscious masculine element in women. Jung said that we need to connect with that part of ourselves in order to achieve healthy psychological growth.

Often when we choose a partner we recognize the anima or animus in the other person and are attracted to it as a way of reclaiming that 'lost' part of ourselves. Modern psychological thought assumes that people have both an anima and animus and when they suppress or fail to recognize this internal 'opposite' it is expressed by 'projecting' itself onto others.

Projecting needs onto others

The mechanism of projection is a major player in relationships on many levels, so it is important to explain the workings of this complicated but everyday psychological phenomenon. The term is usually used to denote a situation in which people disown or reject feelings in themselves which they find distasteful or unbearable and locate them instead in someone else.

A good example of this occurred when, over a period of weeks, a friend of mine would phone me up and during the conversation would say: 'You sound really depressed, John' or 'You sound quite down.' At first her comments played on my mind, but then I realized it was almost certainly a classic case of projection.

The next time she phoned and said 'You sound depressed, John', I responded. 'No, Mary, I'm not depressed at all. Maybe it's you who's really feeling that way. Do you want to talk about it?' After a silence, Mary admitted she had been feeling quite low for some time and had not wanted to acknowledge it.

Similarly, if a person is feeling bored or unfulfilled within a relationship they might begin to have fantasies of an affair, but find the idea so shocking that they attribute these feelings to their partner, imagining that the partner is looking around for a liaison outside the relationship. This type of projection can often reach a point where one party accuses the other of flirting or being unfaithful to cover their own thoughts of infidelity.

The term projection is also used when people attribute qualities to another person which they would like or need them to have. The classic example is the idolization of celebrities, whereby people imagine the object of their adulation to have the attributes of a god or goddess, projecting superhuman qualities onto them when they are in fact just ordinary people who happen to be in the spotlight.

This kind of projection occurs frequently in the early stages of a relationship and often before it has even begun. We see someone and make instant assumptions about them based on our early experiences as children (more about that later in the book); or we imagine they have the qualities we are looking for in a potential partner based on our own needs.

 A perfect working example of this kind of projection was offered to me by an insightful client of mine named Joanna. She had been in an increasingly unhappy relationship with a man named James for some two years. During the course of our sessions together she had been able to recognize that she was with him because initially he had appeared to be everything she was not, that is to say emotionally strong, confident in social situations, and capable of making instant decisions when faced with a difficult situation.

It transpired that James was in fact quite weak emotionally and extremely lacking in self-esteem, but he had become very good at covering it up by bluffing his way through situations and putting on a mask of confidence. When the cracks began to show, Joanna found herself with someone who was almost the opposite of what she first assumed.

She was also able to acknowledge that James reminded her of her rather pathetic father, and she had been drawn to him because of a parental 'transference', the psychological term for when we experience a throwback to a familiar situation (more about transference in Chapter 10).

Joanna was eventually able to wean herself off the relationship and leave James. Shortly before she ended therapy with me, she said: 'I looked at a photo of James the other day and realized that he wasn't the person I was with'. Joanna was acknowledging the desperate need she originally had for James to be the kind of person she wanted him to be, when he was in fact quite different. She had projected those sought-after qualities onto him, but as soon as she was able to take off her rose-tinted spectacles she was able to move on.

A dangerous quest

As you can see from that case study, this form of projecting is a dangerous if very human thing to do. In the quest for someone to complete you, it is all too easy to think that you have found that special person when you know them only in a superficial way. The expression 'love at first sight' has a lot to answer for!

To know someone fully and deeply, to understand their emotional make-up, and their positive attributes, as well as their foibles and fears, usually takes years. And yet people rush headlong into relationships because the need for that wonderful new person to be everything they want them to be can be overwhelming, especially if they are feeling lonely and unloved.

Far more important than the need to become one with someone else is the need to become one with yourself. As

I was at pains to stress earlier, only you can fulfil your emotional needs and heal your emotional wounds. A partner can help, but in the end the person you have to live with and answer to is yourself. Learning how to do that is the subject of the next chapter.

- Try to recognize when you are making assumptions about a new partner based on qualities you would *like* them to have.

- Take time to get to know a prospective partner in as much depth as possible before committing to them.

- Ask searching questions if necessary. It may save you from heartache later on.

- Accept that you and you alone can bring about your happiness.

Keep in mind this quotation from Neale Donald Walsch: 'The purpose of relationship is not to have another who might complete you, but to have another with whom you might share your completeness'.

---

3. All by myself

*All men's miseries derive from not being able to sit in
a quiet room alone.*
Blaise Pascal

The need to find our other half has another dimension, which is often put forward by experts in the field of relationships as a primary cause of falling in love. This phenomenon happens when two people meet and there is an overwhelming attraction or 'chemistry' between them.

When this special kind of connection is made there is a feeling of merging with the other person. There is no me or you, just a wonderful feeling of being one, of being able to go beyond our normal limits, physically and emotionally. To put it another way, there is a feeling that our personal boundaries have been erased and our sense of self has become fused with the other person. In psychological terms this is known as 'the collapse of ego boundaries'.

In his admirable bestselling book *The Road Less Travelled*, Scott Peck says: 'It is because of this collapse of ego boundaries that we may shout at the moment of climax "I love you" or "Oh, God" to a prostitute for whom moments later, after the ego boundaries have snapped back into place, we may feel no shred of affection, liking or investment.' This is a somewhat extreme example, but it gives an idea of the emotional power this sense of merging can unleash.

Freud's 'omnipotence' theory

The reason we find this letting go of personal boundaries so attractive, and in many cases hypnotic, is that it represents a kind of psychological bridge back to the idealized state of early childhood. In the early stages of development outside the womb a baby is unable to see any distinction between itself, the world around it and the other humans who inhabit that world.

Because of this, the baby develops a sense that he is 'master of the universe', a belief that he is able to control everything because he is universally connected; he is one with his mother, his surroundings and anyone or anything else that comes within his sphere of awareness. Sigmund Freud, the founder of psychoanalysis, referred to this as the 'omnipotent' stage, when an infant believes his thoughts can change the world around him. Freud stated that this illusion is dispelled through the experience of 'frustration', which is a feature of the 'reality principle'.

So, for example, the baby might think: 'When I get hungry and I cry, my Mum always appears and gives me food. But Mum is really me, so I'm the one who's really making it happen.' This sense of total power is lost when the infant begins to realize that he is in fact separate from everyone and everything, most notably his mother.

This is a huge loss which never completely disappears even in adulthood. It is hardly surprising that we try to rediscover that sense of merger and magical power, when anything seemed possible and we lived in a world where our every need was, in most cases, instantly catered for. And one of the most obvious ways we can do that is by merging with another adult in a love relationship.

Attachment theory: to boldly go

It is fair to say that the most important developmental task for any child is learning how to survive alone in this world – in other words how to give up relying on his or her parents for support and become independent. If a child does not negotiate that transitional stage successfully, they will usually encounter problems in later life, with a likelihood that they will be plagued by insecurity and dependency issues, especially in their adult relationships.

Developing healthy independence stems from having a reliable, nurturing relationship with the adult who is chiefly responsible for basic early care giving, such as feeding, giving affection and generally responding to the infant's needs. In most cases that is the child's mother, but it can also be the father, a close relative or someone outside the family, depending on circumstances. That individual is known as the 'primary caregiver'.

The importance of good bonding with the primary caregiver as a platform for emotionally healthy adulthood is the basis for one of the major theories of developmental psychology known as 'attachment' theory, originally formulated by John Bowlby in the late 1960s and 1970s. Bowlby's work was further developed by Mary Ainsworth.

As described above, attachment theory concerns the quality of the infant's relationship with their mother or other primary care giver. If the little one develops a sense that their mother will always be there for them, which includes an inbuilt trust that she will always return even if she is absent for a period of time, they develop a sense of security which is carried into adulthood.

Bowlby referred to this as: 'A lasting psychological connectedness between human beings'. On the other hand, if the mother appears unreliable or non-nurturing they will become anxious and fearful, a state of mind that also filters through into adulthood.

Ainsworth identified three types of attachment. The first is known as 'secure attachment', in which a child feels sure that the caregiver will return, even though they feel some distress when they leave. The second category, 'ambivalent attachment', refers to a scenario where a child becomes extremely distressed when separated from the caregiver, usually because they do not make themselves available on a regular basis. Thirdly, there is 'avoidant attachment', where children who received minimal or abusive care show no preference between a caregiver and a stranger because no bond has been formed.

- Try to remember back to the earliest times you spent with your mother and/or other caregiver. If you have no 'direct' memories, your overall impression will suffice.

- Do you think you developed a sense of security or insecurity through their attitude to you?

- Has this sense been carried through into adulthood in terms of how you feel about yourself in this world?

- Do you think these positive or negative feelings affect the way you are in relationships?

People who did not form a secure bond with their primary caregiver – and it is also my belief that we should never downplay the part of the secondary caregiver, e.g. the father – almost always have some form of insecurity when they become adults, which frequently manifests in a needy way of relating to others. They often carry around an ongoing hope, or even a belief, that this deficient caregiver will eventually change and become the kind of parent they would have liked them to be.

When this insecurity is overwhelming or feels like a void that can never be filled, it results in a skewed view of relationships, whereby an individual sees them as essential to their emotional well-being. In extreme cases they may be seen as a lifeline, because the individual feels that they literally cannot survive without being part of a couple.

Relationship addiction

These people will chase relationships, rushing from one to another, often plunging headlong into one that is totally unsuitable just so they can avoid the pain of being alone. This type of relationship neediness is known as 'addictive love' because it has the characteristics of other addictions such as alcohol, drugs and gambling. Psychologists usually list the main features of addiction as:

- Loss of willpower: an inability to control or limit the particular addictive behaviour; in other words the individual develops a morbid, all-consuming dependency or compulsion.

- Harmful consequences: the out-of-control behaviour causes physical or emotional damage to the addict.

- Unmanageable lifestyle: everything else in the addict's life becomes chaotic to a greater or lesser degree because the addiction takes priority.

- Tolerance or escalation of use: the addict needs more and more of whatever it is that he or she craves.

- Withdrawal symptoms upon quitting: emotional and/or physical pain and suffering when the addict tries to give up the craving.

In terms of relationship addiction, I would add to this list the process of 'magical thinking', that is to say, a belief that a relationship will bring about an instant 'cure' for all of life's problems and difficulties (this is similar to a baby's omnipotent thinking, as described above). The love addict idealizes and compulsively pursues someone; then blames them for not fulfilling their fantasies and expectations, before moving on to the next one.

Characteristics of co-dependency

The psychological condition known as 'co-dependency' is a version of addictive love that involves being in and maintaining a relationship that is emotionally cruel, demeaning and/or destructive. Co-dependent people tend to be drawn to and caught up in 'toxic' relationships, in other words to become deeply involved with people who are unreliable, abusive, emotionally unavailable, or extremely needy. Co-dependency is often a form of 'learned behaviour' that is taken on within the context of a dysfunctional family (one in which serious emotional/psychological problems exist but are not acknowledged). Characteristics of co-dependent people include low self-esteem, addictive personalities, and a tendency to be self-sacrificial, adopting 'caretaker' or 'martyr' roles in which they focus totally on the other person's needs and dismiss their own.

Charlie came to see me for therapy because he was suffering from depression and anxiety. An outwardly successful city whiz-kid, he was 'cross-addicted' to relationships, recreational drugs and gambling. During the course of therapy, he was able to acknowledge that his addictions were an unconscious form of self-harm, whereby the damage he did to himself was a way of confirming his underlying belief that he was 'a worthless piece of shit', a description used by his abusive, alcoholic father (his mother was also alcoholic and abusive to him).

Besides frittering away his extremely large salary on gambling and drugs, Charlie stumbled from one abusive relationship to the next, with virtually no gap between them. These relationships were often with other addicts and frequently became violent and emotionally destructive. Charlie told me that when he was without a relationship he feared that he would literally fall to bits and cease to exist; even a violently abusive relationship was better than none and temporarily allayed that fear.

This fear was based on his experiences of appalling childhood neglect. Besides physical and verbal abuse, his parents would leave him on his own from a very early age as they pursued their self-centred, alcohol-fuelled lifestyles. Babies and young children need physical as well as emotional 'holding' from their primary caregiver in order to develop a sense of security and worth, and Charlie received neither in any shape or form.

Donald Winnicott, one of the foremost authorities on child development, talked of the 'threat of annihilation' if the mother's care giving is not 'good enough'. Winnicott also spoke of the infant's 'unthinkable anxieties', which included 'falling forever' and 'going to pieces', as a result of inadequate caring. These unthinkable anxieties echoed Charlie's fear of falling to pieces and ceasing to exist. His desperate need for a relationship at all times was his attempt to fill the black hole that had been left by his parents' total lack of care.

Everyday addictions

It is arguable that we are all addicts to some degree, in the sense that it is human to become obsessed or fanatical about a hobby, an interest or material 'stuff', and to devote disproportionate amounts of time to such things at the expense of more important matters in our lives. For example, a man who becomes addicted to golf might find himself with a marriage that is in danger of falling apart because his wife has become what is known as a 'grass widow' and is feeling neglected.

Besides the traditional addictions of drink, drugs and gambling that I have mentioned, it has become common to hear people nowadays speaking about addiction to chocolate, sex, computer games, television, shopping and a host of other things which feature in modern lifestyles. These 'addictions' do not usually fulfil the psychological criteria I listed and are more accurately habits or low-level compulsions because the loss of control and the self-harm is less severe.

Fear of being alone

In terms of relationships, there is one common factor which applies whether it is genuine addiction or simply a constant craving, motivated by the feeling that something is missing if you are not part of a couple. This is the fear of being alone, and, in the more extreme cases, of being unable to survive alone.

Winnicott states that an infant's capacity for being alone and feeling content with that situation comes from 'being alone in the presence of mother'. He adds: 'Thus the basis of the capacity to be alone is a paradox; it is the experience of being alone while someone else is present.'

So, if a child's mother does not give them the right conditions, namely security, nurture and approval, to enable them to feel relaxed without being dependent on her presence, they will not develop a capacity for being comfortable with themselves and by themselves. As an adult they will crave company and relationships and will get into them for the wrong reasons.

Saying 'Boo!' to the ghost of loneliness

Divorce recovery groups have become increasingly popular in recent years. Many of them take the participants through the various post-divorce stages such as denial, guilt, anger and bitterness, loss and grieving, and letting go. The aim is to work through feelings of loneliness and arrive at a state of what is often called 'aloneness' where you feel comfortable being alone.

One of the best-known divorce 'gurus' Bruce Fisher, examines what lies behind this fear of being alone in his book *Rebuilding When Your Relationship Ends*. Talking of the need to reach a place where you feel genuinely content being on your own and doing things alone, without the need for a partner by your side, Fisher describes the fear of loneliness as a 'ghost'.

He goes on to highlight people who try desperately to escape from their loneliness by throwing themselves into work and/or leisure activities 24/7. He describes them as follows: 'They are running from themselves – as though a frightening ghost lurked inside, a ghost of loneliness.'

The first part of Fisher's quotation, which talks of people 'running from themselves', provides the key to understanding and dealing with this deep-seated fear. People dread being alone because they are frightened they will not be able to handle it. They are so busy trying to avoid the situation that they do not know what their fear is really about. In this context, the well-known quotation by former American president, Franklin D Roosevelt, comes to mind: 'We have nothing to fear but fear itself'.

Fisher suggests that the only way to deal with this fear and reach the desired state of aloneness is to confront it head on: 'Start by facing the ghost of loneliness and realizing that it is a ghost! You have run from it, feared it, avoided it. But when you turn to that ghost of loneliness and say "Boo!" often the ghost loses its power and control. You have accepted loneliness as part of being human, and thereby become more comfortable being alone.'

This is the crux of the matter in terms of developing a healthy and lasting relationship. If you go into a relationship in a highly needy state, looking to your partner to end your loneliness and fill the void inside, you will almost certainly demand more than your partner can give and might eventually drive them away. We might say that, ironically, the essence of togetherness is being apart, which is the basis for our next chapter.

- Get in the habit of spending time alone, doing things on your own, and going to places on your own, whether you are in a relationship or not.

- Try to view being alone as an adventure, not an ordeal; as an opportunity to get to know yourself and be better equipped to know what you want in a partner.

- Keep a diary of what it felt like to 'go solo'. What was negative and positive about the experience?

- Discuss the experiences with your partner if you have one.

You will never be fully content in a relationship until you are happy being alone with yourself.

---

4. Growing together, apart

Love does not consist in gazing at each other, but looking outward together in the same direction
Antoine de Saint-Exupéry

Being in a successful relationship means different things to different people. For many it involves the kind of merging and 'full-on' togetherness talked about in the previous chapters. In pursuit of this desired state of oneness with a partner, some people try to build an exclusive private world in which they live a kind of sealed existence with their partner, doing virtually everything together and, as far as is practical, shutting out the rest of humanity.

The French philosopher, Jean-Paul Sartre, famously said: 'Hell is other people', but these avoidant individuals take his words to an extreme. Their relationships can never be based on genuine respect and unconditional love because there is always so much fear of 'dangerous' outsiders bubbling beneath the surface.

Couples who cling to each other like limpets are often referred to as 'living in each other's pockets', describing a situation where other people are seen as irrelevant, a nuisance and/or a threat to their little corner of heaven. This view of outsiders as a threat to the stability of the partnership is the key to understanding what this unhealthy type of relating is all about.

These fear-based relationships can be likened to two trees that grow together and become fused, so they can never fully reach up towards the light. People who become involved in this type of relationship are almost invariably insecure about themselves, and by extension their partner, often to the point of paranoia.

There will be more about the self-esteem factor later in the book. Suffice it to say in this context that insecure people have an inbuilt belief that they are not truly lovable. Because of this they are plagued by an ongoing anxiety that their partner will meet somebody else and leave them, and therefore they try to keep their partners as close to them as possible at all times.

On the surface, this need to be constantly in the company of the beloved can appear to be a genuine expression of caring, when what they are really doing is exerting subtle pressure on their partner to minimize the time he or she has on their own. So, when their partner goes off somewhere, they might say things like: 'Come back soon; I miss you when you're not here' or 'Every hour we're apart is torture.'

During my psychotherapy training, a fellow trainee described a situation he encountered with one of his clients, which, although it had a degree of humour, took fear-based relating to the highest point on the scale. His client was a married man in his thirties, whose wife tried to keep track of his every move. She would phone him at his office several times a day, ostensibly to say she missed him and couldn't wait for him to return home after work.

She never accused him of being unfaithful directly, but she would constantly ask him who he had been with when he was away from her; whether it was a work colleague or a friend; and ask what they did when they were together, demanding a detailed response with times and places. Her intrusion into his life had reached a point where it was forcing him into a corner and, although he still cared for her on one level, he told my colleague that he was seriously considering leaving her as he could not stand the pressure any more.

My colleague initially suspected that his client might be exaggerating the extreme level of suspicion and interference he described, but he was left with little room for doubt when the wife appeared at his door one afternoon. To my colleague's astonishment, the wife asked if she could sit in on her husband's next session, saying that she felt it would be useful because she could give her own view of whatever his issues were.

My colleague told her that one of the fundamental principles of therapy is that it is strictly confidential, that is to say the material discussed will never be divulged to another party (professional supervision is one notable exception to this rule). On hearing this the wife, in all seriousness, asked if she could hide in a cupboard in the therapy room during his next session!

The paradox of control

As this bizarre episode reveals, fear and its partner in crime, jealousy, can do strange things to people. A degree of jealousy is healthy and normal, especially in the early stages of a relationship when lovers are so besotted with the object of their desire that they cannot bear to be apart from them.

Healthy jealousy shows that we have an emotional investment in the relationship; in other words that we care about our partner and are affected by their behaviour, as opposed to being indifferent, which is usually a sign of a crumbling relationship. It is when healthy jealousy tips over into irrational possessiveness that problems begin.

In its extreme phase, possessiveness can lead to attempts to control a partner's every move so they do not have an opportunity to be unfaithful. However, the great paradox about control, especially when it becomes an obsession, is that it usually achieves the opposite of what it is trying to do. When jealousy becomes all-consuming and one partner tries to invade the other's private space and control them totally, it will frequently make them feel suffocated and prompt thoughts of wanting out.

The absolute extreme in control is murdering the beloved so that they can never become involved with anyone else again. 'If I can't have you, no one else will', is a common theme of so-called 'crimes of passion'. George Bernard Shaw put it this way: 'When we want to read of the deeds that are done for love, whither do we turn? To the murder column.'

Jealousy as 'self-harm'

On a purely physical level, jealousy can make us ill because when we are in the grip of extreme levels of anxiety, which is what jealousy amounts to, our bodies react adversely. Amongst the effects are increased heart rate, high blood pressure, and changes to the blood supply which can, in turn, affect the digestive system.

The psychological effects of anxiety include fear, irritability, heightened alertness, being constantly on edge, and being unable to relax or concentrate, which can eventually lead to stress, depression and panic attacks. Coping mechanisms, which are ways of trying to alleviate these problems, can include drinking and smoking more, or taking drugs, and generally acting in ways that are more harmful than helpful to ourselves.

When seen in this light, jealousy amounts to a form of self-harm, especially when it begins to affect our lives in more general terms. We might find it harder to concentrate at work, become excessively touchy and engage in rows with family members, have difficulty sleeping, and find that recreational activities and hobbies no longer hold any attraction because everything is focused on what our partner is doing, who he or she is with, and what they are doing together.

The irony is that these intense and all-consuming feelings that constitute jealousy at its most powerful are usually based on an illusion. Most of the time it is our own feelings of insecurity that spark irrational jealousy, so what we think we see or know about our partner's flirty or unfaithful behaviour is just a distortion of reality. It is said that 90 per cent of the things we fear in life never happen, but by being unreasonably jealous about a partner we sometimes ensure that fear becomes reality by heaping on the pressure and driving them into someone else's arms.

- Using a scale of 1–10 (10 being the highest), rate yourself in terms of jealousy in your current/previous relationship.

- Using the same scale, how much do you fret and/or become anxious/suspicious when your partner is away from you?

- Do you imagine them flirting, and/or being unfaithful if they are in an environment where there are people you regard as potential rivals?

- Do your own fears and insecurities affect the relationship in terms of unfairly accusing your partner or trying to control them?

Jealousy, or 'mate-guarding', to use the anthropological term for shielding one's partner from the attentions of another, has always been a fundamental characteristic of human behaviour for one sound practical reason. Warding off challenges from predatory males or seductive females was originally a protective response built around reproduction.

Men kept other males away from their mates for the simple reason that it prevented these rivals from impregnating them. If a rival did manage to make the woman pregnant it could mean that he unknowingly brought up a child who was not his own, investing time and resources in the other man's offspring.

Male infidelity did not affect a woman in terms of rearing and nurturing someone else's child, and the loss of social standing was usually less, but it did mean that she potentially lost out on various resources that her man diverted to the child of another woman.

Jealousy as an individual response

This primitive mate-guarding instinct can be said to be the basis for what we know as jealousy but, in psychological terms, there is much more to this gut-wrenching human emotion than reproductive benefits and losses. Jealousy is often preceded by the word 'sexual', and the thought of our partner having sex with someone else explains a large part of what we feel when a partner is the object of a flirtatious rival or initiates the flirting.

However, it is far too simplistic to talk of the sex itself as being the only basis for these feelings, because jealousy is an individual emotion based on the character of the person concerned and their emotional history. So, while there is a common denominator in terms of the instinctive reaction to the threat of a rival, each and every one of us will respond to a situation in subtly different ways.

For example, if someone has a history of failed relationships, where their partner has always been the one to leave, or where they have been unfaithful, that person will inevitably be more sensitive to the possibility of that happening again and will have their mate-guarding 'antennae' on full alert. This kind of individual might do such things as putting prospective rivals down or keeping their partner away from places where there are potential mate-stealers, like social gatherings.

Differing gender responses to betrayal

Gender also plays a part in jealousy, although, as I have said before, I am keen to stress that we should always be careful to avoid stereotyping based on gender. A study by David Buss and colleagues at the University of Texas showed that there are some fundamental differences between men and women in terms of what causes the highest levels of jealousy.

Students were asked to imagine their partner having sex with someone else and then them being in love with that other person. Whilst both sexes found the basic idea of betrayal distressing, a far greater proportion of women (87 per cent) were upset by the idea of emotional betrayal as opposed to sexual betrayal.

Conversely, 63 per cent of male students found the thought of sexual infidelity more upsetting than the emotional form of betrayal. These figures were underpinned by research on physiological responses, such as heart rate, carried out by the same team, which confirmed the emotion-sexuality split between men and women.

As I suggested earlier, trying to keep your partner under control and away from situations where they could be attracted to someone else usually has the opposite effect. Intensive mate-guarding does not work in the long term; the bottom line is that if someone is going to be unfaithful they will do it anyway, either because they are incapable of committing to one person in an ongoing relationship or because there is something fundamentally wrong with the current relationship.

Being open to experiences

If individuals suffering from paranoid jealousy could stand back from their fears, they would see that the closed nature of their relationships also denies them the opportunity of positive experiences through interacting with other people. This is healthy and necessary and can only enhance a relationship in the long term.

The more we bring into a relationship, the more depth and variation there is to it; and, above all, there is freshness and aliveness. If a couple's experiences consist purely of the interactions between the two of them there is little chance of them growing as individuals. And growth is arguably the hallmark of a loving, nurturing relationship, whereas stagnation creates unfulfilled and dissatisfied individuals and ultimately eats away at the fabric of the partnership.

In this context the well-known saying 'If you love someone set them free' is highly appropriate. Genuine love and caring in a relationship means wanting only the highest good for the other person, enabling them to reach their full potential, and not attempting to hold them back as they pursue what they need to make them fulfilled and happy.

Having said that, if someone becomes totally immersed in their own dreams and pursuits, it can potentially be as counter-productive as 'locked in' togetherness. Like so many things in life, it is a question of balance, and getting the balance right is a matter of communication and respect.

Keeping your distance

In order to appreciate your partner fully, you need to maintain a degree of separateness. Being too close to them means you cannot see the bigger picture; there is an inevitable tendency to focus on their human failings rather than their uniqueness and their overall worth. And, of course, being apart, even for a short time, can make the coming together again much sweeter.

The Bohemian poet, Rainer Maria Rilke, put it beautifully when he said: 'Once the realization is accepted that even between the closest human beings infinite distances continue, a wonderful living side by side can grow, if they succeed in loving the distance between them which makes it possible for each to see the other whole against the sky.'

A more famous passage on this subject, one which is often read out at weddings, comes from *The Prophet* by Kahlil Gibran:

> *Let there be spaces in your togetherness.*
> *And let the winds of the heavens dance between you.*
> *Love one another, but make not a bond of love;*
> *Let it rather be a moving sea between the shores of your*
> * souls …*
> *And stand together yet not too near together:*
> *For the pillars of the temple stand apart,*
> *And the oak tree and the cypress grow not in each*
> * other's shadow.*

This is an admirable philosophy, but putting it into practice is not always easy. Many people start out in their relationship genuinely intending to maintain a healthy, loving freedom that ensures growth, but when the challenges of life, as well as potential rivals, loom large, all the good intentions in the world can go out of the window. One major factor in this difficulty is change, both in individual terms and, by extension, to the relationship. We will examine the implications of change in the next chapter.

- Try to recognize when your jealousy is reaching an unmanageable/unreasonable level and talk about it honestly with your partner.

- Accept that there is a basic truth in the old saying 'Absence makes the heart grow fonder.'

- Try to keep in mind that your partner chose to be with *you* and not the hundreds of other potential partners out there.

Trying to chain your partner to your side will only make them see the relationship as a prison.

5. All change, please

We are not the same persons this year as last; nor are those we love. It is a happy chance if we, changing, continue to love a changed person.
W. Somerset Maugham

Fear is the basis for so much negative, self-defeating human behaviour. It is certainly a major cause of disharmony and distress in relationships, where it often lurks beneath the surface, prompting people to act and speak in ways they later regret.

As we saw in the previous chapter, fear of a partner leaving or being 'poached' by another can lead to irrational jealousy and possessiveness that can actually prompt the very thing we dread. This in turn is often underpinned by a fear of not being good enough for your partner or adequate for their needs.

The fear of being alone makes some people seek a partner, sometimes compulsively or addictively, simply because they cannot bear the emptiness they feel when they are not in a relationship. Any relationship, even an abusive one, is better than facing up to the great void which they fear will engulf them if they remain on their own.

Negative perception of change

However, perhaps the most common and destructive kind of fear is the fear of change. This arises when one partner changes something in their lifestyle, such as their career, or something about their personality, which affects the dynamics of the relationship, or at least is *perceived* as affecting it by the other partner.

I have deliberately emphasized the word 'perceived' because the way the other partner regards the change is usually more significant than the change itself. Human beings are creatures of habit; we like stability and predictability. So, even the smallest change by one partner can throw the other one into a state of anxiety where they are gripped by all kinds of fear-based imaginings about how the relationship will be affected.

But here is the crucial thing about change – *it will happen whether you like it or not*. And, as the quotation by Somerset Maugham at the beginning of this chapter suggests, it is not just situations that change; people change as inevitably as the Sun coming up each morning.

- Draw a large circle and divide it in half. In the top half of the circle, write down all types of change that you regard as positive; in the bottom half, list examples of negative changes.

- Next, make a list of the changes that have taken place to you as a person over the past ten years.

- Using a scale of 1–10, with 10 being the highest level of positivity, rate whether these changes have been for better or for worse.

- Using the same scale, assess how these changes have affected your relationship(s).

There are some people who believe that not changing in personal terms is a good thing; that staying the same shows they are reliable and trustworthy. For these people, the idea of change is unthinkable because they do not know how to deal with it; they see it as threatening and destabilizing both to themselves and to their relationships.

The trouble with putting your head in the sand and pretending that a change is not happening – whether that change is to you or your partner – is that sooner or later you will be forced to acknowledge it because it will affect you, your place in the world, your relationship or all three. So, the first principle in dealing with change is to acknowledge it, try to understand why it is happening, and then accept it.

Understanding and acceptance as an antidote to fear and suspicion formed the basis of my work with Sally and Jim, a middle-aged couple who suddenly found themselves caught up in an unfamiliar scenario of conflict and failing communication.

Jim was a freelance journalist and had worked almost exclusively from home for the past 15 years. Sally, meanwhile, had spent most of the marriage bringing up their two children, Joe and Catherine, who had recently both left home.

Sally had become used to having Jim around constantly, but, out of the blue, a former colleague offered Jim a position as public relations manager of a high-profile publishing company. This meant Jim was suddenly out of the house five days a week and sometimes part of the weekend as well.

Sally's reaction was to become withdrawn, uncommunicative and sulky, which mystified and angered Jim and led to them coming to see me for therapy sessions. It transpired that Sally was desperately afraid that Jim, who was a good looking, youthful man, would meet someone younger and more exciting than she was whilst he was in this 'buzzy' environment.

During one of our sessions, I asked Sally what would make her feel more secure about this change. She replied that knowing more about Jim's working environment and what he did there, as well as meeting some of his colleagues, would ease her fears. Jim readily agreed to this, which in itself was a positive sign for Sally.

Sally had come from a family where change was seen as negative and unhealthy, but, having brought her fears into the open, she was able to accept that this change in Jim's work situation could be positive for their relationship because he felt more fulfilled. She eventually found a part-time job herself and they both discovered the benefits of embracing change as part of an ongoing, maturing relationship.

Just like the ghost of loneliness, the only way to deal with change is to face it head on. In *Who Moved My Cheese?* Dr Spencer Johnson offers a simple summary of the steps involved in dealing with change in a positive way:

- Change happens
- Anticipate change
- Monitor change
- Adapt to change quickly
- Change
- Enjoy change
- Be ready to change quickly and enjoy it again and again.

Change is for life

From the moment we are born we change continuously – physically, emotionally, in our behaviour, and in our outlook on life – as our experiences and relationships shape our world view and our attitude to the big issues of living.

Research on the functioning of the brain has shown that external experiences actually change its structure. A team of scientists at the University of California, Los Angeles (UCLA), led by neuropsychiatrist Jeffrey Schwarz, performed PET scans on eighteen OCD (Obsessive Compulsive Disorder) patients before and after ten weeks of mindfulness-based therapy.

Twelve of the eighteen showed marked improvement. Significantly, their post-treatment scans revealed that activity in the orbital frontal cortex of the brain, the core of the OCD circuit, had fallen dramatically, leading Schwarz to comment: 'Mental action can alter the brain chemistry of an OCD patient. The mind can change the brain.'

This ground-breaking piece of research shows that the world and the experiences it presents to us have a clear and measurable impact on our personalities. In other words, we cannot stay the same even if we want to. And the key question is: why would we want to?

Life as a 'flowing process'

Carl Rogers, one of the pioneers of modern psychotherapy, and founder of the person-centred approach to therapy, stressed that people are continually changing and evolving. Rogers regarded change and openness to new experiences as the essence of human happiness and fulfilment.

In his book *On Becoming a Person* he writes: 'Life, at its best, is a flowing, changing process in which nothing is fixed … I find I am at my best when I can let the flow of my experience carry me, in a direction which appears to be forward, toward goals of which I am but dimly aware … Life is guided by a changing understanding of and interpretation of my experience. It is always in process of becoming.'

The flowing process that Rogers speaks of is a natural part of human development. Our personalities, our way of being in the world and our general outlook on life alter as we move from childhood through adolescence and into adulthood. But becoming an adult does not mean the changes stop there; far from it.

Life events – especially major ones such as career changes, the beginning and end of relationships, the arrival of children, the death of family members, and religious or spiritual epiphanies – can, and usually do, bring about huge changes in people.

These changes can be disturbing and destabilizing, both to the individual concerned and their partner. The key to dealing with these major shifts in one's life is always to attempt to see the positive in the change, even if it simply means taking on board the old cliché, 'When one door closes another opens.'

In practical terms, this means talking about the changes, and seeing them as an opportunity for growth for the individual concerned and for the relationship. This sharing of new directions and new experiences can bring a couple closer together, because even though it is only one person who is in process of change, going through it together can bring a sense of closeness and intimacy.

The inevitability of change

Of course there will be some experiences that are hard to view positively in any way, such as being made redundant, or the death of a loved one. But even here, the only way forward is to mourn the loss and move on. Although it is hard to accept when we are in the middle of something hugely distressing, life is a series of losses which we must negotiate in order to retain a healthy perspective which will allow us to move on to the next phase.

These inevitable losses include the different and necessary stages of life we must go through. For example, the loss of one's youth is a huge blow for many people, but rather than seeing it purely as a loss, we can welcome new opportunities offered to us in our later years, such as the freedom to travel, and to try new pursuits, and, with people living longer and staying healthier, even embarking on new careers.

Changing one's career or job can be one of the major destabilizing factors in a relationship. As the case study of Sally and Jim showed, when one partner changes their work situation, it can have enormous implications for the relationship, especially if the other partner feels threatened or resentful.

Becoming parents

The birth of children brings change on many levels. The parents are no longer just John and Maggie, or whoever; they are now John and Maggie plus one, or two; and that has major implications in terms of how they see themselves as individuals and how they relate to each other.

Suddenly, there is a new life, a new member of the family, and that is wonderful and enriching. But the 24/7 demands of a baby can put a huge strain on a relationship, especially when the parents are deprived of sleep. A new baby also means a loss of freedom and spontaneity in terms of the ability to do things together as a couple.

Many people also find themselves overwhelmed by feelings of responsibility for the welfare of the tiny, helpless individual who has appeared on the scene. And bringing up children is a costly business; a couple's finances can be stretched by the financial demands of clothing and education, which can also put pressure on the relationship.

If the male partner is insecure on a personal level or in the context of the relationship itself, it is not uncommon for him to experience feelings of jealousy at the bond between mother and baby. Often this manifests as a sense of being 'pushed out' or relegated to second place in his partner's affections.

Variations in sexuality

Changes in sexuality are inevitable. People's need for sex varies on an individual basis, from day to day, and over time. There is a whole chapter on sex later in the book, but the point to stress here is that in an ongoing relationship, a couple's way of relating sexually *will* change.

Nowadays, the physical side of sex is highlighted at the expense of the many psychological factors operating below the surface, which is misleading in the extreme. How someone is feeling emotionally has a huge effect on their sexuality; in fact, the two things are inextricably linked. So, for example, if someone has lost their job, suffered a bereavement, or is feeling anxious or depressed, that will usually result in a lowering of their sex drive to some degree.

The original chemistry that draws two people together can never remain at that peak of physical intensity; and following on from this, our need for sex on a regular basis usually changes as we age. In many cases, affection and companionship can become as or more important than physical intimacy, although, of course, each case is individual.

Illness can mean change in a couple's sex life, and it can also affect the relationship itself on a profound level. One partner may become incapable of engaging in interests and pursuits that were once shared, or they may need looking after on an ongoing basis, which, no matter how loving and caring the healthy partner is, inevitably puts a strain on both individuals.

'The price of doing the same old thing'
All of the changes listed above mean there will be a shift in a couple's way of relating to each other, which involves altering on a personal level to meet the demands of the change. This can sometimes seem too scary and overwhelming to

contemplate, which is why people choose to deny the change or become hostile to it.

However, if we can see these changes as an opportunity to grow together and to revitalize the relationship, rather than seeing them purely as a trial or an obstacle, it can enhance and strengthen the bond between partners. In the final analysis, it is stagnation, not change, that is the real enemy. As Confucius said: 'They must often change, who would be constant in happiness or wisdom.'

So, how do we ensure that change is beneficial in practical terms? The first, and in many ways the only, rule is always to acknowledge the change and discuss it honestly and openly with your partner. The importance of genuine communication between partners cannot be over-emphasized, which is the subject we move on to next.

- Accept that change happens.
- Face the fear connected to the change.
- See change as a new horizon, not a dead end.
- Talk to your partner about any change.
- Get used to change by making a habit of it!

Lack of change means stagnation, which can damage a relationship by default. Staying the same is not an option.

---

6. Are you receiving me?

Two monologues do not make a dialogue.
Jeff Daly

If there is one word that should be engraved on your mind when you embark on a relationship it is 'communication'. The importance of this thirteen-letter word that trips so lightly off the tongue but weighs heavily on so many relationships cannot be over-stressed. It is no exaggeration to say that all the principles in this book can prove meaningless if there is a lack of proper communication between partners.

The first thing to say on the subject of communication is that when most people think they are communicating they are not; at least not in a way that brings about a genuine meeting of minds and therefore enhances their relationship. As the quote from Jeff Daly above suggests, communication needs to be a two-way thing. To have any benefit it has to be a dialogue in which information is given and received in a spirit of cooperation, as opposed to one party simply getting across their point of view, or just 'scoring points'.

Effective communication involves two separate functions: talking and listening. To have genuine significance, these two functions should be seen as complementary and inseparable. However, in terms of maintaining a healthy relationship, listening is the greater, more rewarding skill because without listening, in the sense of truly trying to understand what is being said, the person doing the speaking might as well be talking to the wall.

The truth is that most of the time when we communicate, whether it be to friends, business colleagues or spouses and partners, we are so keen to make our point or speak our truth that we do not give a full and fair hearing to their response – and in some cases we do not want to hear it. They in turn are so busy preparing their response that a stalemate situation is set up before the presumed dialogue even begins!

Revealing statistics about listening

The following statistics from the International Listening Association should make us stop and think seriously about our ability to listen in a meaningful way:

- When we think we are listening, most of us are distracted, preoccupied or forgetful for about 75 per cent of the time.

- We think at 1000–3000 words per minute, but listen at only 125–250 words per minute.

- Marketing studies indicate that the average attention span for adults is 22 seconds, which is why television commercials usually last 15–30 seconds.

- Immediately after we listen to someone, we only recall about 50 per cent of what they have said.

- Long term, we only remember 20 per cent of what we hear.

When people train to be a counsellor or psychotherapist, the art of listening is often the first skill to be taught. This is because listening means so much more than just sitting opposite someone and trying to take in everything they are telling you. One of the reasons for this is our attention span, which as the statistics above reveal, is restricted on average to a matter of seconds rather than minutes.

Truly focusing on someone else's words without our attention wandering to some degree does not come naturally, which is why student counsellors have to be trained in the art of listening to clients and maintaining their attention for the full duration of sessions that usually last for 50 minutes or an hour.

In terms of adult love relationships, this kind of focused listening also means becoming truly selfless by training ourselves to be other-focused rather than self-focused, and trying genuinely to understand what our partner is attempting to communicate. At the same time we must be able to bracket our own issues and responses no matter how much they are demanding to be aired.

- The next time you have a conversation with your partner, a friend or a work colleague, try to notice how often your mind strays to your own agendas whilst they are speaking.

- Once you become aware of your mind straying, try to push your own agenda(s) to the back of your mind and really focus on the other person's words and what they are trying to convey to you.

- On a scale of 1–10, rate yourself on how different your ability to listen becomes when you genuinely try to hear what they are saying, compared to when you are preoccupied with your own issues or busy formulating a response in your head (give yourself two scores, i.e. 'before' and 'after').

As part of developing listening skills, students of psychotherapy and counselling are taught to develop the skill of 'active listening'. This means focusing on the other person on more than one level, and includes the capacity to observe as well as listen, and to reflect back to them, as well as merely hearing the words on a superficial level. This also involves observing a person's body language or facial expressions, taking in the whole picture of that individual.

In attempting to understand the message or story they are trying to get across it is important to notice if there is any contradiction between what they are saying and how they appear. For example, they might be saying they feel fine about a particular situation but at the same time they might look irritated or angry. In this case something is usually being suppressed.

Communication: maker or breaker

Rather than offering a specific case study to illustrate this chapter on communication, I would prefer to say that when people reach crisis point in their relationship, it is almost *invariably* because of a breakdown in communication. My own work with clients, both as individuals and couples, brings this point home time and again.

The root cause of their problems will usually revolve around personality clashes, and/or differences in the way they view major issues such as sex, child care or finances; but in most cases it is their inability or unwillingness to talk about those problems, to listen to their partner's viewpoint, or failure to receive a proper hearing from their partner, or a combination of these, that brings the relationship to a 'make or break' situation.

An unwillingness to listen, or more accurately to *hear*, what the other person is trying to get across creates a vicious circle of resentment and, as a result, an even greater restriction on communication and, eventually, a total shutdown. Pride, fear and a perceived loss of self-esteem are usually at the root of this downward spiral (self-esteem is the focus of the next chapter), with a reluctance to back down and thus to be seen as weak often driving the spiral of negativity.

Once a relationship has become mired in conflict and communication has become increasingly strained, the downward spiral can be difficult to break because problems tend to become self-perpetuating. In other words negativity breeds negativity, so lack of proper communication leads to even worse communication or none at all.

The element of time

In modern relationships, problems with communication are often made worse by a lack of time. It is true that if we really want to communicate with our partner we will make time, but people are faced with such an array of competing demands from all sides these days, that they are often too exhausted or emotionally drained to get involved in 'heavy' or meaningful communication, which can be seen as just another pressure.

In her book, *Anatomy of Love*, Helen Fisher refers to modern 'commuter marriages', in which couples live some way from each other and commute to meet as and when possible. I would suggest that the term can also be applied to modern relationships in which two people live together but lead such hectic lifestyles, with full-on careers, children to bring up, social lives to pursue, and 101 other tasks to shoe-horn into their week, that communication in any real sense often becomes nothing more than an elusive dream.

Decoding non-verbal communication

Research on listening processes has shown that couples in unhappy marriages and relationships find it hard to 'decode' or interpret non-verbal communication from their spouses. The overall state of the relationship affects the way messages and behaviour are interpreted. Individuals in relationships that are going through difficulties are more likely to interpret ambiguous or unclear communication and behaviour in a negative way.

Contrastingly, people whose relationships are going well will use a more positive lens for interpreting those same behaviours and communications. Problems with decoding may also affect an individual's perception of how their partner is supporting them.

Another factor that lies behind poor communication, and one that never ceases to amaze me no matter how often I come across it in my client work, is the expectation of 'mind reading' by one or both parties. The feeling that a spouse or partner should somehow know what you are thinking without it being said is an extraordinarily common phenomenon. Furthermore, people often do not realize they have this expectation, and when it is pointed out to them they are taken aback, go into denial mode, or even become embarrassed.

It is true that couples who are together for a lengthy period of time develop an instinct for what their partner is thinking, but to expect the other person always to be able to divine your thoughts is unrealistic and dangerous. This false expectation can be used unconsciously to undermine or get at the other person; that is to say, assuming they should know what you are thinking, then attacking them when they do not.

The 'unheard' party will often play hurt or sulk because they feel they have not been listened to, despite the fact that they have not vocalized their feelings in the first place! This kind of behaviour can also be motivated by feelings of low self-esteem, which in turn become unconscious attention-seeking in an attempt to get their partner to notice them and engage with them.

- Are there occasions when you make assumptions that your partner knows what you are thinking? Be as honest as possible about your answer.

- Try to recall specific instances of those 'mind reading' expectations.

- If you had not had those expectations, would it have resulted in a different and/or more positive outcome to that particular situation?

- How would you have felt if you had voiced your feelings openly and honestly instead of putting the onus on your partner?

On one level, the simple truth is that communication is not rocket science. How can the other person know what you are thinking or feeling if you do not say it out loud? And how can issues be resolved if they are not spoken about honestly and openly with a full disclosure of feelings, fears, and concerns, and given a fair hearing by the other party?

Having said that, it takes courage to be totally honest and open because it is human to hold something back, if only to protect our pride and limit our vulnerability, and also because a grievance aired by one party can be seen as an attack on the other. The crucial factor in dealing with what appears to be negative communication is not to go automatically on the defensive and take it as a criticism, but rather to evaluate objectively what is being said. And always bear in mind that your partner has a right to his or her feelings, no matter how different or contradictory they might appear to your own view.

Following on from this, when feelings have been brought into the open, the next stage in the process of genuine communication is discussion, followed by negotiation and compromise, whereby both parties look at how they might move from entrenched positions without losing face. When there has been a genuine attempt to listen on both sides, both parties know that their feelings have been validated, even if there has been nothing more than an agreement to disagree.

'Core conditions' for communication

There used to be signs on British trains saying 'In case of emergency pull communication cord'. Those words could be seen as a mantra for couples experiencing relationship emergency. But merely pulling the cord, in other words trying to communicate when things reach a crisis, is usually too little too late.

Desperate attempts to bridge a gulf that has become a great divide often do not work and can occasionally make things worse. People need to be taught how to communicate properly as a matter of course, not merely to go through the motions, and sadly that teaching is not usually available.

The psychologist Carl Rogers, who was mentioned in the previous chapter in connection with change, stipulated three 'core conditions' for successful therapy – **empathy**, **congruence** and **unconditional positive regard (UPR)**. These core conditions, which I will now explain briefly, can be used as a basis for successful communication in adult love relationships. For the purposes of this exercise, I have substituted the word 'partner' for Rogers' use of 'client'.

Empathy: trying to put yourself in your partner's shoes and understand what they are feeling. In other words, to see the world – and your relationship – through their eyes.

Congruence: being genuine or real in your attitude and responses and not offering a false picture of how you see your partner (although there are times when discretion and diplomacy are necessary).

Unconditional positive regard: being non-judgemental and seeing your partner as a valuable human being despite their faults and human weaknesses.

Rogers originally stipulated six core conditions, which were later condensed into these three. One of the original six was 'making psychological contact' with the person to be helped. In my view, making psychological contact encapsulates the other three conditions and is arguably the key factor in developing meaningful communication.

The essence of psychological contact is 'tuning in' to your partner in a way that enables you to understand them and care about what they are going through. We might find it hard to empathize or sympathize in every situation, but trying to put yourself on the same wavelength is a first step.

The next step is accepting that they have weaknesses and shortcomings; that they can be hurt; that they mess up and do not always get it right; that they are, in a word, human. Often what we find hard to accept or forgive in someone else is something we find unacceptable about ourselves.

The point of no return
If one party cannot or will not hear what their partner is trying to communicate, is not willing to understand or at least

try to understand what is going on, and is not prepared to accept and move forward, or at least try to do this on some level, then I would say there is little hope for that relationship. This also applies if one party is not prepared to open up in some way and disclose what they are feeling, especially if it is having a negative impact on the relationship.

As I said earlier, everyone keeps something back, which is not necessarily a bad thing, and there will be times when it is hard to be totally open and honest. However, if something important and potentially damaging to a couple's closeness and mutual respect and caring remains unsaid, the foundations of the relationship are in danger of being undermined. And if those unspoken feelings are allowed to build up, a parting of the ways may become inevitable. The message is clear: stop, look and listen!

- Always try to put aside your own agendas and responses when listening to what your partner is telling you. Your turn will come!

- Being honest about your feelings should be seen as a strength, not a weakness.

- As it says in the Bible, 'Do not let the Sun go down on your anger'. Talk about your negative feelings before they turn to resentment and potentially create an even bigger problem.

- Do not leave attempts at meaningful dialogue until the relationship is in crisis.

- Make a specific time, or times, to communicate, no matter how busy your week, and try to keep channels of communication open at all times.

 Communication is a two-way process. Without proper listening, communication means nothing.

---

7. The self-esteem factor

The state of your life is nothing more than a reflection
of your state of mind.
Dr Wayne Dyer

Self-esteem plays a huge part in determining the quality of our relationships. How we feel about ourselves in terms of positive and negative self-image is inevitably played out in our interactions with our partners. So, the quotation from Wayne Dyer above could readily be altered to read: 'The state of your relationship is nothing more than a reflection of your state of mind.'

Imagine you have had a dressing-down from your boss. After work you go for a drink with a colleague who says he's heard unofficially that another colleague is going to be given the promotion you had set your sights on. Your self-esteem would be flagging badly. Then, when you finally arrive back home, a neighbour sees you walking miserably into the house and asks: 'Is everything okay? You don't look well at all.'

On a scale of 1–10, your self-esteem would probably be down in the 2 or 3 area as you walked through the door. One more negative communication would put you close to zero, ready to hide away from the world. As you pour yourself a large one and slump down on the settee, your partner appears looking serious and says: 'There's something we need to talk about.'

Whatever this 'need to talk' involves, you will be on the defensive right away. As a result of your bad day, you are feeling undermined, sorry for yourself, and your self-esteem is at such a low point that it has all but disappeared. Is your partner likely to receive a fair hearing for whatever they have to say? Will they feel the rough end of your tongue or be treated to an impression of the Incredible Sulk? You do not need to be an expert in human nature to provide the answers.

Now, imagine the same scenario with your partner after you have had a great day at the office and a series of positive communications from colleagues and friends. Unless your relationship is at or approaching the end point, it is fairly safe to say that under these wholly different circumstances, i.e. when your sense of self-worth is high, your readiness to listen to your partner and your willingness to be empathic and to compromise would be far greater.

Oprah Winfrey once said: 'What we are trying to tackle in this one hour is what I think is the root of all the problems in the world – lack of self-esteem is what causes war because people who really love themselves don't go out and try to fight other people.' Following this line, people who are feeling good about themselves do not usually pick fights with their partners, undermine them or respond to them unfairly or harshly.

- Imagine you have had a bad day for whatever reason(s) and your self-esteem has taken a serious knock. Then try to picture yourself in a challenging situation with your partner.

- Ask yourself how much your flagging self-esteem would affect the quality of your communication with your partner.

- Do you think that under the circumstances you could be sympathetic/empathic and fair when listening to and evaluating what they have to say?

- Try to recall specific occasions when your self-esteem was low, you did not listen to your partner and responded in an unfair or negative way.

- Compare these to the times when you felt good about yourself and were able to listen and respond in a fairer and more positive way.

You might have noticed that I have been speaking about self-esteem being 'high', 'low' and 'flagging', which gives us one major clue about the nature of self-esteem: it is fluid and forever changing. It is also controlled and influenced by what are sometimes referred to as our 'foundational beliefs', that is to say the fundamental views we hold about ourselves, which shape our character and personality.

Most experts now believe that a person's character is based on a combination of nature and nurture; meaning our genes and how we were treated as children. I agree with this, although I tend to emphasize the importance of the latter more, being of the opinion that whether we are extrovert or introvert, optimistic or pessimistic, secure or insecure, is determined more by our parents or primary caregivers than our biology. Other factors, such as pressures from society and media 'brainwashing' play a part too, of course.

If we are repeatedly told negative things about ourselves, put down and ridiculed, it will inevitably make us insecure and anxious. In other words, our foundational belief about ourselves will centre round such statements as 'I'm a loser', 'I'm stupid and clumsy' or 'I'm unlovable'.

On the other hand, if those who care for us in our early years (and, to a greater or lesser extent, in the later stages of our childhood and our adolescence, too) constantly praise us, validate our feelings and make us feel lovable, it is likely that we will grow up to be confident, well-rounded adults, far less prone to anxiety and depression, and with a 'glass-half-full' or 'can-do' attitude rather than 'glass-half-empty' or 'can't-do'.

In this context, the famous poem by Dorothy Law Nolte comes to mind. The following is an abridged version:

Children Learn What They Live

If a child lives with criticism, he learns to condemn.
If a child lives with shame, he learns to feel guilty.
If a child lives with encouragement, he learns
confidence.
If a child lives with acceptance and friendship, he learns
to find love in the world.

The type of character you have directly correlates with your self-esteem because you will have developed assumptions about the way the world is. For example, if you are an optimist you will think everything will work out for the best, and therefore you will tend to handle seemingly negative scenarios, such as losing your job or a relationship break-up, relatively well.

This is in contrast to a pessimist, whose assumptions of negative outcomes mean he will tend to blame himself when things go wrong, regarding them as part of his 'life script'; or he will take it as confirmation that his lack of worth as a human being means things are destined to go badly for him

A model of low self-esteem

Dr Melanie Fennell, a clinical psychologist at the Oxford Cognitive Therapy Centre, has developed a model of low self-esteem; how it is triggered and how it can lead to depression and anxiety. In basic diagrammatic form, the model looks like this:

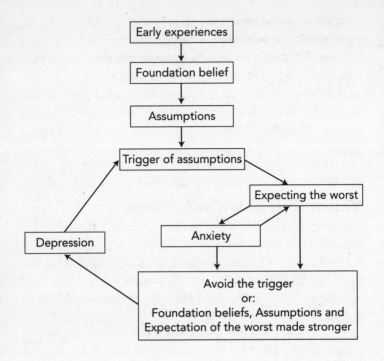

A point I am keen to emphasize is that within the limits of our 'pre-set' character, which makes us who we are as individuals and serves as a starting point for our self-esteem, there is room for movement. Furthermore, it is fair to say that the fluctuations in our self-esteem are continuous, depending on the daily circumstances of our lives – sometimes they can even vary from hour to hour. As the 'bad day' example just illustrated, these fluctuations colour our mood and our outlook and almost invariably affect the way we react to our partners.

Another key factor about self-esteem is that we are constantly striving to maintain it. Unless we happen to be one of those rare people who do not worry at all what others think of them (I am not certain that anyone is totally devoid of this anxiety), the way we *believe* we are perceived by others is crucial to the way we see ourselves and feel about ourselves.

Vicious circle of low self-esteem

The emphasis on the word 'believe' indicates that what we assume to be true is often not the reality at all, but because we believe it to be so, it affects us deeply. And what we believe can lead to a vicious circle of self-criticism and condemnation, because if our self-esteem is already at a low point we will be more ready to soak up negative messages about ourselves whilst at the same time filtering out any positive ones.

In this context, a visualizing exercise used in CBT (Cognitive Behavioural Therapy) is worth mentioning. If someone is stuck in a loop of negative thinking, the therapist will ask them to imagine they are a post box with a traditional rectangular opening. Negative messages are seen as rectangular so they can be accepted through the opening; but positive messages are circular so they do not fit. The therapist uses this image to help the client become aware of their resistance to taking in positive messages, and will help them to train their mind to become aware of when this is happening so they can change the pattern.

It is arguable that we are always monitoring our self-esteem in any given situation, be it at work in our dealings with colleagues, when we meet new people in social settings, in conversations with friends, dealing with professionals such as doctors and teachers, or with people who serve us in shops and restaurants. And, of course, in our relationships.

Our concerns about maintaining our self-esteem are largely centred around not being seen as weak, inadequate, or wrong. So, in the case study featuring Bill and Angie in the introduction to this book, the couple's constant battles took an immediate turn for the better when they were able to acknowledge that their vicious circle of fighting and 'hitting back' was, to a great extent, about trying not to appear vulnerable or lose face.

- Think of yourself holding a conversation in any situation – e.g. work, social setting, discussion with your partner. Would your communications and behaviour be influenced by trying to look and sound a certain way?

- How much would you be concerned about how the other person is seeing you and evaluating you?

- How important would it be for you to be seen as possessing certain qualities and characteristics and, following on from this, not to be seen as incompetent, inadequate, or lacking in some way?

- Are the previous points connected to a perceived loss of face and/or loss of self-esteem?

A third point to note about self-esteem is that we often project negative feelings about ourselves onto others, thereby setting them up as critical or judgemental when, in reality, the criticism is coming from our own mind. The psychological mechanism of projection was looked at in Chapter 2, but here is a quick reminder: it is an unconscious process whereby we offload difficult or unacceptable feelings about ourselves by locating them in someone else.

Projection can be a major player in relationships where one or both partners are suffering from self-esteem problems. For example, if someone's self-esteem is low because they are feeling unattractive or inadequate in some way, they might believe that their partner no longer fancies them and withhold affection or withdraw sexually. Or if one partner is feeling sexually frustrated and begins looking around lustfully at other people, they might try to deal with those 'unacceptable' feelings by seeing their partner as the one who has wandering eyes, or even accuse them of having an affair.

Low self-esteem is also responsible for 'self-fulfilling prophecies', another unconscious psychological mechanism, in which we bring about or 'set up' circumstances we fear without realizing we are doing so. After the negative scenario has occurred, the person who brought about the self-fulfilling prophecy will often say something like: 'I knew she would eventually leave me, and now it's happened exactly the way I predicted.'

Mark was a successful investment banker, outwardly confident, sociable and popular. However, he had a history of abandonment – his father left when he was four; his mother died when he was six (which was in effect another abandonment); and his wife left him for his best friend after just three years together – which made him deeply insecure and unsure about his value as a person and also his 'manliness'. To add to those major personal losses, Mark had been through a long series of relationships with women who had always ended up leaving him after relatively short periods.

When Mark came into therapy with me he had re-married and had been with his new wife almost two years. Although it had lasted far longer than his previous brief relationships, this second marriage had gradually deteriorated to a point where his wife was threatening divorce.

During our sessions, we examined Mark's deep-seated insecurity and low self-esteem and how it might be playing into his new marriage. After a lengthy period of attacking his wife's character and denial of his part in the conflict, it transpired that Mark was constantly flirting with other women, had become increasingly distant and aggressive towards his wife, and had withdrawn from any kind of intimacy.

When I pointed out to him that he was behaving in a way that was calculated to drive his wife away – a self-fulfilling prophecy in action – Mark initially reacted angrily towards me. However, he then became very emotional and said: 'I guess you're right; that's what I do, and I do it every time, but I feel powerless to stop myself.'

I explained to him that his behaviour was unconsciously designed to bring about the very thing he feared – i.e. his partner leaving him – because then he could tell himself something like, 'I knew that would happen because I'm worthless and people don't want to know me', thus confirming his low opinion of himself.

Working towards self-acceptance

Recognizing how your lack of self-worth is affecting your relationship is a first step, but dealing with it in a way that makes it more manageable and helps you build a more positive self-image is something that often requires professional help from a counsellor or psychotherapist.

A therapist from the more traditional schools, such as psychoanalytic or psychodynamic, will take you back to your childhood to try to establish the roots of the low self-esteem, and may help you to recognize negative voices or an 'inner critic' (often a belittling parent) that re-surface in the present and keep you stuck in patterns of negative thinking.

With CBT (Cognitive Behavioural Therapy) the focus is more on the 'here and now' and involves looking at faulty 'cognitions' (thoughts) which, although they represent a distorted version of reality, keep being replayed. For example, if you have a belief that people find you boring you will convince yourself that you are dull and uninteresting whenever you are in a social situation and unconsciously avoid others. They, in turn, will see you as stand-offish and keep away from you, confirming your conviction that people do not find you interesting.

The aim of therapy is not to become totally immune to negative thoughts about yourself, because that is unrealistic; the goal should be more about self-acceptance, focusing on your positive attributes, and being aware of negative thinking that becomes self-perpetuating.

As can be seen from the case study involving Mark above, low self-esteem that is not dealt with can be destructive and even if it does not destroy a relationship completely, it can lead to constant conflict, which brings us to the subject of our next chapter ...

- Monitor your feelings and try to see if there is a connection between moments when you feel low, or lacking in confidence, and when conflict happens with your partner.

- Remember your partner is not responsible for your self-esteem. Only you can change negative feelings about yourself and your life. If these persist, arrange to see a counsellor or psychotherapist or go to your GP for help.

- Keep in mind this quotation from Eleanor Roosevelt: 'Nobody can make you feel inferior without your consent.'

Insecurity, self-doubt and poor self-image can bring about the very thing you fear.

8. The meaning of conflict

Whenever you're in conflict with someone, there is one
factor that can make the difference between damaging
your relationship and deepening it.
That factor is attitude.
William James

Because people bring their own unique character and view of the world into relationships, there can be no cast-iron guarantees about the way a particular partnership between two people will work in practice. The one thing that can be safely predicted is that because people are as individual as fingerprints there *will* be disagreements and conflict, by which I mean something more serious and potentially damaging than lovers' tiffs.

It might sound strange to go further and state that conflict not only *will* happen but *should* happen, but if conflict is not present in a relationship it can be said with some certainty that something is being suppressed by one or both partners, and that is not healthy or beneficial. As I explained in Chapter 6 when looking at the importance of genuine communication, withholding feelings or not speaking out about something that is important to you often fosters resentment, which can eat away at the fabric of a relationship and may eventually destroy it.

How arguments can keep a relationship alive

Disagreements can serve as proof that a relationship is still alive and viable. If one partner is not prepared to get involved in a potential conflict situation, it can signify that they have no emotional investment in the partnership. In other words, their passion, love or respect for the other person has died and they cannot find the enthusiasm to engage in battles.

Relationships often hit the buffers because they have lost their spontaneity and excitement and have become mired in the day-to-day routine of life. Because of this people will sometimes initiate conflict (usually in an unconscious way) to test if their partner is still interested enough in them to respond. Insecure people will often do this as a matter of routine to check out their partner's commitment and level of caring.

For some couples, being at war constantly is a way of stimulating the relationship and maintaining a feeling of aliveness. Such people often come from family backgrounds where conflict was routine and was therefore seen as a normal way of relating, so living without the 'white noise' of background rowing seems strange and uncomfortable.

Differences in conflict styles

Psychologists talk about 'conflict styles', referring to the way individuals engage in conflicts. These styles are based on the way conflicts were handled in a person's family. Consistent exposure to a family's individual 'fighting' style will imprint itself on a child's mind and become a template for conflict in adulthood.

For example, one family member might have been completely dominant and imposed their view on the others with a prohibition on any discussion or negotiation; there might have been a climate of bickering and endless disputes, which were never resolved; or there might have been an avoidance of conflict by 'bringing the lid down' as soon as the mere possibility of disagreement reared its head.

'Attachment styles' – the way in which an individual bonded with their mother or primary caregiver, as explained more fully in Chapter 3 – also play a part in relationship conflict. Securely attached people usually have more of a capacity for handling conflict constructively and negotiating compromise with their partner. In contrast, insecurely attached individuals tend to view conflict as more of a threat and respond in less constructive and more defensive or damaging ways.

CASE STUDY

Linda's marriage of twelve years was in serious trouble when she came to see me. A shy, insecure woman in her late thirties, she had long suspected her husband, Tony, was having an affair with a colleague at work and had finally forced him to confess when she found a series of intimate text messages from the other woman on his mobile phone.

During the heated and prolonged row which followed Tony's confession, Linda kept pressuring him to explain why he had embarked on the affair. Questions like 'Is she prettier than me?', 'Is she funnier?' and 'Is she better in bed?' elicited fairly non-committal replies from him. It was only when Linda became more desperate and begged him, 'Please, tell me the reason; you owe me that much' that he finally opened up.

Tony told Linda that he was drawn to his mistress because she seemed more passionate about life and was not afraid to show her emotions, negative as well as positive. For him, that was like a breath of fresh air, or, perhaps more accurately, a breath of life.

It hurt Linda deeply when Tony added that he had always found her unresponsive emotionally; she refused to get involved in arguments by 'dampening them down' as soon as they started. Because of this Tony said he felt that their relationship had become stale and unfulfilling and he no longer found her attractive on a physical as well as mental level.

In our subsequent sessions, Linda revealed that her parents had always instilled in her that showing emotion was wrong. Far better to keep your feelings inside and soldier on no matter what the problem was, they said. For example, even when Linda was bullied at junior school she was in effect told 'Get on with it; that's life', and left to fend for herself.

Positive feelings such as joy and elation were also strongly discouraged, and displays of affection and love had no place in family life at all. It was as if they expected Linda to be a robot, which, sadly, was the way Tony eventually came to perceive her.

Gender differences in handling conflict

Earlier in the book, I pointed out the dangers of gender stereotyping, which sometimes results in the portrayal of irreconcilable differences between the sexes. However, there is some truth in the suggestion that men and women have certain basic variations in the way they handle conflict. For example, research has backed up what is often taken as a given of male–female relationships, namely that when it comes to responding to problems women are more likely to want to talk about them, whereas men will back away from them and put up emotional barriers.

For both men and women, however, the dream of finding someone you are totally in harmony with 24/7 – sometimes referred to as a soul mate – is a misleading fantasy. The reality is that if a good fairy waved her wand and conjured up a dream partner who agreed with you about every little thing, never raised their voice or revealed strong emotions (like the Stepford Wives in the film of the same name) you would almost certainly find them boring and irritating and the relationship would feel more dead than alive – as was the case with Tony and Linda.

TRY IT NOW!

- • Take a pen and paper and make lists of the main features of conflict as you see them, dividing them into 'positives' and 'negatives'.

- • What do these lists tell you about your attitude to conflict?

- • How much does your attitude owe to your family's way of dealing with conflict?

- • Do you see conflict as inevitably damaging to your relationship or an opportunity to put things right and move on?

Conflict is considered a no-go area for many people, not only because they have had it drummed into them since childhood that it is bad to fight and show anger, as in Linda's case, but also because in certain societies it still carries a social taboo to some degree, as with the traditional British 'stiff upper lip', which in my opinion is still a feature of our national character. In other societies, for example among Latin peoples, giving vent to your emotions without holding back is considered normal, which, provided it is not taken to extremes, is the healthier attitude.

As the quote from William James at the start of this chapter highlights, attitude to conflict is crucial in the context of relationships. Conflict that becomes vicious and involves personal attacks is destructive and leads to entrenched positions where the parties are concerned purely with getting back at each other and winning at any cost. That cost is often far higher than they imagined when the conflict began; that is to say, a downward spiral that is difficult or impossible to halt and, eventually, a parting of the ways.

Resolving conflict can enhance a relationship

On the other hand, if conflict is dealt with in a constructive way and all thoughts of winning and losing are put aside, it can offer an opportunity to air differences, which in turn gives people a chance to examine their own views on a particular subject as well as their wider world view and to contrast these views with their partner's. If this is done in a spirit of conciliation, it can enable the parties to negotiate a compromise which can not only bring a satisfactory end to the dispute but can also enhance the relationship.

People grow and mature through dealing positively with struggles and adversity. Those seemingly negative situations are, to use the old cliché, character building, and offer opportunities for change and new possibilities. Resolving conflict in a healthy and positive way can place a relationship on firmer foundations in the long term because it represents a positive shared experience that can serve to foster increased intimacy.

Following on from this, it is important to accept that not all major disagreements will be resolved – nor is it essential that they should be. It takes a degree of humility – that important but so often neglected quality – to give up the need to be right and to concede that the other person's view has merit and maybe even takes precedence over your own view of things (politicians please note!). And sometimes the wisest and most constructive course of action is to agree to differ.

Research on 'perpetual' differences

Research by psychologist John Gottman, who specializes in relationships and, in particular, the factors that influence break-ups, has shown that most conflict in relationships is perpetual (69 per cent). It has no way of being resolved because it is based on fundamental differences in personalities and needs. Couples can either have 'gentle dialogues' about these perpetual issues or they can live in a state of 'gridlock'.

Gottman also found that within each partner's position regarding their 'perpetual' issue, there is what he terms a 'hidden agenda', a nugget of deep and personal meaning for that partner. The reason couples have the same argument over and over again is because their position on a particular issue is linked to deep personal beliefs or values which makes compromise seem impossible.

For example, a disagreement over the frequency of sex within a relationship needs to be looked at in the context of each partner's views of sex generally, and the meanings they attribute to it, which will inevitably be linked to their own personal experiences and their upbringing.

Gottman's research (in conjunction with Robert Levenson) has also identified four components which appear to signpost doom in a relationship. Referred to as 'The Four Horsemen of the Apocalypse', these are:

- Criticism – verbally attacking or belittling the partner

- Defensiveness – claiming their own behaviour was acceptable or justified

- Contempt – showing scorn for their partner

- Stonewalling – refusing to acknowledge or discuss problems in the relationship.

If you examine these four predictors of doom, what becomes clear is that they highlight an 'adversarial' approach to conflict; that is to say a 'win or lose' mentality, together with the lack of any attempt to consider the other person's viewpoint and to work at a compromise. If one party is no longer committed to the relationship and is consciously or unconsciously seeking a way out, they are more likely to engage in a confrontational way; although straightforward pig-headedness can also be at the bottom of such behaviour!

If a relationship is not at or near the 'end game', a middle way of dealing with conflict can arise, in which couples seek to keep things at a level where damage is minimized and they find a way of being together that is workable if not totally satisfactory. Some couples rub along together in this way for years, often with a mixture of resentment and affection that becomes an acceptable way of life.

Pros and cons of maintenance behaviours

These more conciliatory types of solution to relationship conflict are sometimes known as 'maintenance behaviours' and include a willingness to sacrifice or downplay your own beliefs or goals; responding in an accommodating way to your partner's unfair or inconsiderate behaviour; and not viewing the grass as greener and seeking seemingly better alternatives, such as an affair.

Of course, maintenance behaviours can be just a sticking plaster and may not solve the problems in the long term. Gottman says that one of the key factors in dealing with conflict on a lasting basis is gentleness, by which he means a softening of one's approach and attitude to a problem. He also advocates good friendship and intimacy, and suggests that these need to be supplemented by a 'shared meaning system'.

'Partners need to identify and communicate their sense of life's purpose and the meaning they assign to their daily moments,' Gottman says. 'They need to reveal to one another their priorities and values, their goals and missions, their ethics and morality, their overall philosophy of life ...'

Because people have different backgrounds, life experiences and world views it is unrealistic to expect couples to 'sing from the same hymn sheet' on all issues. But, if there cannot be agreement on a particular issue there has at least to be an understanding of the other partner's position and, ideally, a degree of compromise; or, more importantly, a *will* to understand, to try to put yourself in your partner's shoes, and to concede that their point of view is just as valid, if not more so than yours.

Real communication is crucial

Given this kind of accommodating attitude, a spirit of compromise, and gentleness of approach (to use Gottman's word), dealing with conflict in a constructive and healthy way then becomes first and foremost a matter of open and honest communication. As mentioned in Chapter 6, this means listening in a focused, non-judgemental way, as well as talking.

Without this kind of 'real' communication it is impossible to understand what your partner is feeling deep down about a particular issue, what motivates them to approach it from a particular standpoint, what fears they have about abandoning this position, and how it could affect their self-esteem.

To take this further, without open and honest communication you will not be able to develop a full and meaningful understanding of your partner's foundational beliefs about themselves and life, and how they came to hold those beliefs; in other words what makes them the person they are; the person *you chose* to be with.

As I have emphasized more than once in previous chapters, people's reluctance to communicate openly is usually based on fear – fear of losing face and self-esteem, fear of being seen as stupid, weak or vulnerable, or fear of being taken advantage of – and pride, which is fear-based anyway. In order to negotiate conflict successfully, these fears have to be set aside, which takes courage, 'big-heartedness', and a willingness to stand back and see the bigger picture. If your relationship is to last and grow, anything else is not an option.

 • Try to see conflict as a normal component of a relationship, which, if successfully negotiated, can enhance closeness rather than destroying it.

• Agree on what the core problem is; then negotiate steps to deal constructively with it.

• When arguing with your partner, focus on the good of the relationship and avoid criticism and personal attacks at all costs.

• Be as honest and open as you can. Voice your fears and anxieties and listen to your partner's concerns without pre-judging or dismissing them.

- Focus on the present. Let go of old grievances and resentments, which colour your ability to see the current situation in a fair and objective way.

 Dealing successfully with conflict means giving up all thoughts of winning and losing.

---

9. Crazy for you

We are never so defenceless against suffering
as when we love.
Sigmund Freud

The first half of this book has focused on some of the key components that we need to work on to achieve healthy relationships, such as communication, change, and conflict. In order to do this, there is an assumption that we can be rational about these matters. However, in the early stages of relationships, at least, that assumption can be meaningless because any notions of rationality, ordered thinking and healthy objectivity are often tossed straight out of the window.

Taking up the quotation from Freud above, one of the first things we do, if not *the* first thing, when we enter into a romantic relationship is to lower our defences. As mentioned in Chapter 3, the lowering of our personal boundaries, or 'the collapse of ego boundaries', as it is sometimes described – in other words letting the other person in totally, or merging with them – has been put forward by psychologists as one of the primary features of romantic love.

That this leaves us open to suffering, as Freud suggests, can readily be evidenced by the obsessive thinking and extreme states of physical and mental arousal that so often overwhelm us when we embark on a new relationship. This is especially true if that someone we have chosen appears to fulfil all the criteria of the special person we have been searching for, or a 'soul mate' to use the popular label.

Obsessive fantasizing

A conference on love and attraction held in the United States in the eighties, came up with the following highly technical description of the temporary malfunctioning of the mind that frequently affects people when they enter into a romantic love relationship: 'A cognitive-affective state characterized by intrusive and obsessive fantasizing concerning reciprocity of amorant feelings by the object of the amorance.'

Whilst this might sound like a master class in psycho-babble, it contains a nugget of relationship gold that is worth examining in more detail. The key words that can be picked out are 'intrusive and obsessive fantasizing', which accurately describe the out-of-control mindset that is a feature of love's 'madness', loss of perspective and detachment from reality.

I am not suggesting that everyone who begins a relationship is prone to the full extremes of this madness. However, when we meet someone to whom we are instantly and deeply attracted or drawn to strongly, a degree of altered behaviour and thinking on some level is the rule rather than the exception. This in turn means we often do not see the situation – and the person – in a realistic way.

Magic to make the sanest man go mad

The Ancient Greeks referred to love as 'the madness of the gods'; in Homer's *Iliad* it is described as 'magic to make the sanest man go mad'; and Plato said 'all love is divine madness'. Think also of modern day descriptions of love, which include 'I'm crazy for you', 'Head over heels in love' and of course 'Falling in love', which all contain a suggestion of the mind being taken over by a kind of temporary insanity.

The obsessive fantasizing and the compulsive pursuit of this special person we desire so intensely is very much concerned with trying to maintain a level of control over the situation. However, the irony with this 'loved-up' state of mind is that it often brings about the opposite of what we are trying to achieve. When we wait by the phone, check text messages over and over again, or try to imagine what they are doing, and who they are with every second of every day, we are, in effect, *out* of control.

The craziness of the initial phase of a love relationship also involves giving up our power to the object of our passion. With a few whispered words or a loving gesture, this magical person has the ability to 'lift us up where we belong', to paraphrase the title of the hit song by Joe Cocker and Jennifer Warnes. Or, if they do not phone when they say they will, or appear to be paying attention to someone else, they can bring us crashing back down to earth.

CASE STUDY

Marion came to see me suffering from 'low-level' depression; that is to say she was constantly feeling unhappy and tearful, but she was able to carry on with her life and carry out her roles as a single mother of two teenage children and part-time medical secretary – in contrast to people with clinical depression, who are often incapable of functioning on a day-to-day basis.

However, even though she was not immobilized by her low moods, she saw life as one long trial rather than something to be experienced and enjoyed. She said she found it hard to get up in the morning because she lacked any kind of motivation or meaning. But perhaps the most revealing thing she told me during our early sessions was that she felt as if she was constantly searching for something and never found it.

It soon became clear that Marion should have said 'someone', not 'something' because when I asked her to think of what she needed to give her life meaning, she immediately said 'The right man in my life'. She then revealed that she had been in a long series of relationships with men who she initially saw as potential life partners.

Every time she met a prospective partner she would be so consumed by this new passion that she would drop everything else in her life to pursue him. Her work would suffer and, by her own admission, her children would be neglected emotionally as she poured all her emotional resources into her new love.

Initially, the men in her life appeared to be equally keen to have a committed relationship. However, when we looked at why these partnerships were relatively short-lived, it transpired that Marion had behaved in such an over-the-top way – often phoning them twenty or thirty times a day, calling at their homes unannounced, and sending them endless gifts – that she had obviously been perceived as obsessive to the point of craziness, even verging on being a stalker.

When Marion was able to stand back and evaluate her behaviour rationally she could see why these potential 'life partners' only stayed around for such a short time. Our work together then became focused on helping her to bring a more considered, objective approach to future relationships and to try to become aware of the times when she was in the grip of love's madness and therefore acting irrationally and, in a sense, self-harming.

Tennov's theory of limerence

Following her in-depth research into love and relationships in the 1960s, the psychologist Dorothy Tennov coined the term 'limerence' to cover the irrational, obsessive aspects of romantic love we have just mentioned. Tennov's research covered 500 people, both heterosexual and gay, from different backgrounds and age groups, and her findings formed the basis for a book entitled *Love and Limerence*, which was published in 1969.

The characteristics of limerence include: fantasy, intrusive thinking, cognitive obsession, uncertainty, anxiety and an implied demand for reciprocity. Tennov described limerence as addictive, neurotic and delusional, and regarded it as more than mere infatuation.

Being in a state of limerence is similar to the soaring highs and despairing lows which are experienced by people suffering from manic depression (also known as bipolar disorder). Fantasy is a major component, with extreme or even fairytale situations being imagined by the person in the grip of the temporary 'insanity'. For example, they might fantasize that they will rescue their beloved from a terrible fate and in return receive their undying love; or they might believe that the object of their desire can see their every move and hear their every word at all times.

Distortion and denial

When we are in the grip of this initial 'unbalanced' phase, it is common to develop a distorted view of the beloved, whereby all their negative characteristics are denied, and they are imagined to be a kind of Superman or Superwoman, completely immune to the usual human weaknesses and faults. An article on research into the basis for romantic love in the *Journal of Policy Sciences* described the phenomenon of lovers' distortion and denial as follows:

'Romantic love is characterized by a preoccupation with a deliberately restricted set of perceived characteristics in the love object which are viewed as means to some ideal ends. In the process of selecting the set of perceived characteristics and the process of determining the ideal ends, there is also a systematic failure to assess the accuracy of the perceived characteristics and the feasibility of achieving the ideal ends.'

Self-deception can be the most destructive enemy of all. People will go to the most extraordinary lengths to twist, shape and generally manipulate the character of the beloved to make them fit the illusion that they are 'the one'. No matter if the loved one is treating them like dirt, having affairs, sponging off them, or abusing them physically, the deluded individual will not only ignore it all, they will refuse to hear anything bad being said about Mr or Ms Wonderful by anyone else.

Denial is the name of the game and loved up individuals are past masters at it. Admitting to even the smallest flaw in the one who has been sent to them by fate is not even a consideration because it would mean the loss of the dream of perfection. I have lost count of the number of times clients have told me negative, demeaning or shocking things about their partner's behaviour and followed this up with: 'But I love him [or her]!'

Acknowledging the bad behaviour would be hard enough; leaving the relationship is simply not within the realms of possibility, despite the fact that they would actually be making life better for themselves. This is usually based on a fear of separation, a dread of being alone and having to face the world, oneself and one's demons without recourse to 'the other half'.

- Focus on the period after you met someone to whom you were powerfully attracted (it could be your current or most recent partner or someone from the past).

- Try to remember ways in which your behaviour or thinking deviated from the usual (small ways are just as important as major changes). Make a list of those changes.

- On a scale of 1–10, how differently did you act during that first phase of the relationship in terms of thinking and behaviour that was uncharacteristic/fantasy-based/obsessive or a combination of those?

- Did this altered thinking affect your ability to view the object of your passion in a rational/objective way?

There have been many studies of the phenomenon known as romantic love focusing on its power to bring about measurable mental and physical changes. For example, a study by the British Psychological Society, which examined a variety of brain scans, found that the brain 'in a state of love' and the brain 'in a state of mental illness' show a 'considerable overlap'.

Other studies have shown that people who fall in love have symptoms of OCD (Obsessive Compulsive Disorder), such as constantly washing their hands, checking that doors are shut, and performing other minor rituals over and over again. Researchers at Imperial College found that the range of physical effects caused by the ups and downs of romance can cause long-term damage to the human body which equates to stress-induced illnesses.

The 'rollercoaster' sensation of romance examined in the Imperial College study will be familiar to anyone who has experienced the feelings of over-excitement, disturbed sleep patterns, loss of weight, and obsessive thinking that come as part of the deal when we meet someone who presses all the right buttons. And, although it is not strictly within the scope of this book to examine the biology and chemistry of relationships, it seems important to make at least a brief mention of the biochemical, or 'brain chemistry' factors which play a vital part behind the scenes.

Why love makes us PEA-brained

The main chemical protagonist in the drama is known as PEA (phenylethylamine), which leaps into action during the early stages of a relationship. PEA acts like an amphetamine on the brain and the central nervous system, causing them to go into overdrive. Clubbers use amphetamines or 'speed' as it is known, to give them a high which keeps them going well beyond their usual limits; and they used to be the principal ingredient in diet pills because they suppress hunger.

In practical terms, the key factor about PEA in romantic relationships is its capacity for 'hyping up' our thinking and behaviour to a point where we lose our inhibitions and control, lower our boundaries, and act in uncharacteristic, over-the-top ways. PEA also causes the familiar physical reactions which come with the giddy excitement of a new relationship – sweaty palms, pounding heart, butterflies in the stomach, and general nervousness and over-arousal.

When PEA is released into our system, our adrenaline levels increase and this in turn stimulates the release of dopamine, a chemical that is involved with many important human functions. These include behaviour, thinking, movement, and what is known by psychologists as 'reward-based' behaviour, which is often associated with addictions. This is where a reward – usually a good feeling or a high, albeit temporary – is gained from taking drugs or alcohol or engaging in gambling.

The onslaught of the 'love chemicals' on our system does not stop there. When PEA and dopamine are in action they suppress the functioning of serotonin, a nerve chemical which controls our impulses and passionate urges. When the level of serotonin drops, it can make us feel depressed, panicky, obsessive and out of control. People who suffer from OCD, mentioned earlier, have low serotonin levels and are often prescribed Prozac to correct this problem.

To complete the 'chemical brothers' line-up, we have a neuropeptide called oxytocin. Neuropeptides are molecules used by neurons (cells in the nervous system) to communicate with one another. Oxytocin is often referred to as the 'cuddle hormone' and is released by the brain during birth, breastfeeding and sexual activity. During orgasm oxytocin levels soar and our bodies are also flooded with natural opiates known as endorphins, which produce the kind of highs associated with intense physical workouts.

Looking at this list of hijackers lurking behind the scenes (by no means a complete list in scientific terms), we are clearly not masters of our own destiny when we fall for someone. Furthermore, there is a variety of psychological 'drivers', which are out of our awareness or unconscious, that play their part in drawing us magnetically to a particular person, as will become apparent.

- When you enter a new relationship try to step back and observe yourself, your behaviour and your thinking. Are you acting out of character, irrationally or obsessively?

- Try to look beyond the natural high and anticipation that comes with any new relationship and see the bigger picture. In other words, give yourself time and space and ask yourself if this person is right for you in the long term.

- Sensitively reject any pressure from your new partner to take the relationship to a level for which you are not ready.

'Fools rush in', which can be incredibly exciting and life-changing, but can also end in tears.

---

10. The parent trap

The past is not dead. In fact, it's not even past.
William Faulkner

We read a lot these days about the so-called 'law of attraction', referring to the power we supposedly possess to call on the universe to deliver what we need or desire in our lives. In my view, such a phenomenon seems highly questionable; although it can be argued that if you actively and persistently pursue a certain goal or a particular set of circumstances you will bring about the conditions that make this more likely to happen. With this in mind, what about a law of attraction for relationships? Is there such a thing, and, if so, how does it work?

Rather than looking at a formula for attracting the right person into our lives (already the subject of many self-help books), I propose in this chapter and the next to examine some of the underlying factors that lead us to choose the people we choose, and to whom, in many cases, we find ourselves compulsively drawn. Given the diverse range of influences that contribute to our selection of a partner, '*laws* of attraction' might be a more appropriate term.

We have already looked at the biochemical aspects of attraction that go to work when brain chemicals are released into our system and we experience the all-consuming excitement that takes over when we meet someone special or fall in love. Pure physical/sexual attraction is, of course another key player in the game and a very powerful one at that. Indeed, those who hold a cynical view of romantic love maintain that lust pure and simple is the basis for what we know as love at first sight.

Hoodwinked by a trick of the genes

Beneath the hypnotic pull of sexual desire, something even more powerful is going on. When we experience that 'Wow!' feeling for someone across a crowded room, the biological urge to mate and reproduce is kicking in. In *The Road Less Travelled*, Scott Peck says: 'Falling in love is a trick that our genes pull on our otherwise perceptive mind to hoodwink or trap us into marriage.'

Other relationship drivers include cultural pressures, and influence from the media which subtly (or not so subtly) induce us to make the relationship choices we make.

However, given the nature of this book, it is the psychological aspects of attraction that I will focus on in more depth, and in particular the way our parents played their part in creating our 'love maps'. These are the pre-set criteria by which we select our partners based on a whole range of physical, cultural and psychological factors that determine our individual approach.

Connecting through psychological radar

Henry Dicks, a psychoanalyst who became famous for his pioneering work in the field of couples therapy at the famous Tavistock Clinic in London in the fifties, highlighted three main areas involved in partner selection:

1. **Public aspects**, which include social pressures such as class, religion and money; as well as ethnicity, religion and education.

2. **Conscious expectations**, covering values and attitudes, shared interests and physical appearance.

3. **Unconscious attractions**, which form the basis of the instant 'chemistry' between two people.

The great paradox of these love maps is that although they are individual, they often have one major area of overlap with people to whom we are strongly attracted, namely our family background. In simple terms, the way we were raised as children, especially how our parents treated us, gives us a unique psychological template which can act like a magnet to people with similar backgrounds.

For example, if a person was raised in an atmosphere of criticism and condemnation and was constantly belittled, making them an anxious, insecure adult lacking in self-esteem, this will be picked up by the psychological 'radar' of a prospective partner with a similar background. The two people will feel a deep mutual attraction that is based on a kind of instinctive knowing, outside of their conscious awareness. This 'knowing without knowing' is the basis for Dicks' third category, the unconscious aspects of attraction that draw us to people of similar backgrounds.

Power of the unconscious mind

The power of the unconscious mind, which is the basis for psychoanalysis, should never be underestimated. The metaphor of an iceberg is often used to illustrate this: the tip above the surface represents the conscious mind, and the far greater mass below the surface, the unconscious mind.

As well as retaining memories of everything we experience and acting as a control centre for our emotions, the unconscious mind enables us to function on autopilot when carrying out certain tasks such as driving a car, for which 30 different skills are needed. The unconscious mind also controls vital bodily functions including heart rate, blood pressure, digestion, the endocrine system, and the nervous system.

Neuroscientists have shown that the conscious mind provides five per cent or less of our cognitive (conscious) activity during the day; so most of our decisions, actions, emotions and behaviour depend on the 95 per cent of brain activity that is beyond our conscious awareness; that is to say 95 per cent or more of the way we conduct our lives is controlled by the programming in our unconscious mind.

To give a more technical slant on these statistics, Bruce Lipton, a pioneering figure in the world of medicine and biology, has stated that the unconscious mind operates at 40 million bits of data per second, whereas the conscious mind processes at only 40 bits per second!

Not just a face in the crowd

Unconscious attraction has played an important part in the work of the Institute of Family Therapy in London. It was highlighted by family therapist Robin Skynner in *Families and How to Survive Them*, a book he wrote in conjunction with the comedian John Cleese, of *Fawlty Towers* and *Monty Python* fame.

During training at the institute, Skynner asked students to engage in something called 'family systems exercise', which originated in the United States, and was designed to demonstrate the underlying reasons why couples specifically choose each other from a crowd when they have never met before and have no prior knowledge of each other.

The exercise involved trainees being put into groups and asked to choose another person from the group who reminded them of someone from their family, or who they felt might have filled a gap in their family. They were not allowed to speak; they could only move around and visually focus on the others in their group.

When they had chosen someone, they could discuss what made them pick each other. The couples were then asked to choose another couple and made to form a 'family', with each individual playing a role within that family.

They then talked about what influenced them to make their decision before returning to the big group to discuss what they had discovered.

The extraordinary feature of this exercise was that the three people they chose invariably came from families who functioned in similar ways to their own. For example, their own family might have had an absent parent, or an abusive or critical parent; or they might have had certain unwritten rules about expressing emotions, being affectionate or general behaviour; or they might have suffered a major loss or losses, or been forced to cope with a significant life change or changes.

- Make a list of the factors that played a part in attracting you to your current or previous partner.

- Try to break these down into the three categories used by Henry Dicks, which we mentioned on page 123.

- If you find it hard to come up with unconscious reasons (which is perfectly normal) try to think of similarities in your family backgrounds.

- Looking at all these factors, do you think you chose your partner because he/she fitted the requirements of your 'love map'?

Cleese, whose role in *Families and How to Survive Them* is to question the psychological principles from a layman's point of view, asks Skynner about the 'wallflowers', the people who do not get chosen, and the fact they appear to constitute an anomaly. However, Skynner says that the wallflowers actually clinched the argument because in the very first group of twenty trainee therapists who carried out the exercise under his supervision, it transpired that the members of the group who came together last had been fostered, or adopted, or brought up in children's homes, and had therefore been made to feel rejected early on in their lives.

This blind attraction might seem hard to accept for those who have not experienced it, but, as already explained, the power of the unconscious mind is quite uncanny. Furthermore, the pull of the unconscious does not stop at family background in a broad sense; for a variety of reasons, we are also drawn to people who remind us of a parent.

Childhood love replayed

This is where another major element of unconscious attraction enters the picture – the psychological process known as 'transference', a pioneering discovery by Sigmund Freud. Freud noticed that several of his younger female patients appeared to be falling in love with him, but he was astute enough to realize that this attraction was not based on his personal magnetism, but was a throwback to the patient's childhood when 'Daddy' was their first object of love.

That 'love', Freud realized, was being transferred to him in the current situation, albeit a professional one. Freud was later to claim that all love is transference love, an interesting viewpoint which gains credence when we look at transference in an everyday setting.

Transference occurs in many different situations as we go about our daily lives. Indeed, it has been said that we never see people as they truly are. Authority figures are frequent triggers for this kind of distortion. For example, when we have an appointment with a doctor or a teacher, or if we have to appear before a judge, that person might remind us of a parent who was strict and remote with us and we therefore respond to them in a similar way.

'Repetition compulsion'

Sometimes we choose partners because there is 'unfinished business' with a parent that needs to be worked through. For example, if a girl's father was neglectful and unloving towards her, she might unconsciously choose a partner who reminds her of him in an attempt to get him to love her the way her father never did.

When transference occurs in the guise of unfinished business, the attempt to set things right can lead to an endless cycle of fruitless searching and 'replaying'. Freud used the term 'repetition compulsion' to describe this human tendency to repeat situations that are familiar to us, even if they are harmful.

The classic example is children of addicts, who often end up in a relationship with an addict, and frequently move from one addict to another. To escape from the cycle of self-destruction seems impossible because whilst moving to a more healthy type of relationship might appear attractive on one level, it represents unfamiliar territory and is therefore quite scary.

Early mother love as a template

It is now widely accepted that the template for our adult relationships, both in terms of sexuality and love, is formed in early infancy and even, it has been claimed, in the womb. This happens through our early sensory exchanges with our mothers, especially when breastfeeding is involved, and is carried on and amplified through the different stages of interaction with our parents.

Scientists have found that the biochemical and neural signals which bring about bonding between an infant and its parent are the same signals which are activated when we meet a prospective mate. It has also been shown that when starry-eyed lovers gaze at each other they are re-enacting the bonding looks between mother and baby, which psychologists term 'eye love'.

It is normal for children to see the opposite sex parent as a 'love object', not only because they have nurtured them emotionally and physically (even in cases of neglect or abuse there can still be a perverted kind of love), but also because that parent gives them their first experience of adult masculinity or femininity – 'He's big, he's strong, he'll protect me', or 'She's sweet and soft and nurturing'. Part of that experience is what it means to feel sexual attraction, although in the vast majority of cases that attraction remains 'safe' and does not get acted out.

The 'Facebook of attraction'

For cynics who remain unconvinced about this unconscious parental magnetism, there is scientific evidence to back it up, which is literally 'in your face'. David Perrett, a psychologist at the University of St Andrews in Scotland, carried out research into factors that make people's faces attractive to us.

Using a special computer morphing system, Perrett took images of students' faces and transformed them into the opposite sex. They were then asked to choose the most attractive face from a selection of different images. Of all the faces they were shown, the students always chose the adjusted image of themselves, even though they did not know that it was their own face disguised.

Perrett concluded that people find their own (morphed) faces attractive because they remind us of the faces we looked at constantly when we were children – that of the opposite sex parent. This goes a long way towards explaining why, when we are powerfully drawn to someone, we often feel that we already know them even though we have never met them before. So it is understandable that new lovers often say: 'I feel I've known you all my life.'

Jeff had been through two broken marriages and had been deeply involved with a woman named Maggie for some three years when he came to see me. A good looking, highly intelligent man who held a position as chief executive of an independent television production company, Jeff came across initially as a self-confident go-getter, whose success in business owed much to his dynamic and natural leadership (he had been a captain in the Army before going into the commercial sector).

It soon became apparent that Jeff's business persona was not replicated in his home life. He was totally subservient to Maggie, whose frequently unreasonable and aggressive demands, both practical and emotional, he strove desperately to meet at all times, at the expense of his own needs.

Jeff told me that he felt weak and pathetic, as well as quite depressed, because he was unable to stop himself giving in to Maggie's bullying, and therefore saw himself as 'less than a man'. He wanted to leave but was scared of 'messing up' yet another relationship and plunging himself back into the loneliness and emptiness of the single life again at the age of 55.

When we looked back at Jeff's marriages it transpired that both his wives had been similarly demanding and hostile towards him, albeit in different ways. It soon became apparent that they – and Maggie – were very much like his critical, bullying father, whose demands for academic and sporting excellence were such that Jeff was never good enough.

Jeff had unconsciously chosen replicas of his father because the situation was so familiar to him that it was, in a perverse way, his comfort zone. He was trying to please these women in a 'throwback' attempt to win the approval of his father.

- When beginning a relationship, try to establish if there are similarities in family background that drew you together.

- Bring these similarities out in the open and discuss them with your partner.

- Ask yourselves how you see these similarities playing out in your relationship in the long term.

- Think about your partner's character. Is there any way he/she reminds you of a parent? If so, is the similarity something positive, or is there a possibility that you might be seeking to complete unfinished business?

IF YOU REMEMBER ONE THING

When you start a new relationship take time to get to know the territory. Your love map does not always take you to the place you expect to go.

11. Why opposites rarely attract

*My wife and I no longer have anything in common
but our differences.*
Oscar Wilde

The melting pot of physical, biological and psychological ingredients responsible for drawing one person to another makes the workings of human attraction one of the great mysteries of life. The strands of attraction are so complex and intricate that each and every relationship has its own unique storyline. Small wonder, then, that the joy, the sorrow and the drama of love and desire have been the inspiration for countless books, movies and songs.

In the previous chapter we looked at some of the unconscious factors that underpin attraction, notably parental influences and family situations. But does the pull of similarities stop at family backgrounds, or do we find ourselves drawn towards people who are similar to us in other ways?

A common misconception

Opposites attract. This old saying can be said to contain a grain of truth in a superficial way, but generally speaking it is the similarities – whether they are obvious and known about, or hidden or unconscious – that form the basis for attraction between two people.

That said, there is an obvious basis for attraction when we meet someone who seems to be different from us in ways that excite and inspire us. For example, let us say that Karen is a quiet, self-effacing person lacking in self-esteem; it could be uplifting and seductive for her to meet Joe, who is super confident and outgoing, and sweeps her along on a tide of positivity and enthusiasm for life.

This kind of relationship fit can work well if the differences are complementary. To put this another way, people are sometimes drawn to a prospective partner because they see a repressed or 'disowned' part of themselves in the other person, so they choose that person to complement their personality.

This can be positive if they use the situation to recognize and develop that repressed side of themselves and to become a more rounded, psychologically balanced person. However, this scenario often becomes a kind of vicarious living, whereby the partner is used subconsciously to express what they cannot express and to act in ways they cannot.

Furthermore, because the qualities they were attracted to in their partner were qualities they denied or belittled in themselves, this can sometimes mean that in the long term these desired characteristics become distasteful or even repulsive to them. So, after a period of living with Joe's extrovert behaviour, Karen might well find it annoying and even intolerable.

When funny turns to immature

Research at the University of California highlighted the way that qualities which are regarded as positive in the initial phase of attraction between two people can eventually be seen as negative and even despised. The study involved 300 students who were asked to focus on the most recent relationship they had been involved in that had ended.

The students rated characteristics that attracted them most to the other person and those that they found least attractive. The qualities most likely to be admired and subsequently loathed were 'exciting', 'different' and 'easy going'. Carrying on this theme, 'confidence' became 'arrogance', 'funny' was seen as 'immature', and 'spontaneous' became 'weird'.

Even a character trait that might universally be regarded as a given for a successful relationship, such as 'caring', was later seen in many cases as 'possessive'. The stronger and more magnetic the characteristic seemed at first, the more likely it was to become a source of annoyance. And when a personal quality was described as 'unique' it was three times more likely to be one of the reasons for a break-up.

For the complementary fit to work on an ongoing basis, the balance of difference must usually be retained. So, returning to the earlier example, let us say Karen goes to counselling and becomes more confident and outgoing, that would constitute a major change in the dynamics of the relationship.

Joe might feel threatened by Karen's new found confidence, which could have major implications for their 'cosy' life together. She might start going out more, and begin a new career, which could lead to conflict and eventually a break-up if Joe cannot adapt.

Complementary attachment styles

One area where differences can be powerful in a complementary sense concerns styles of attachment (the ways in which individuals bond with their mother or primary caregiver). A person who never received proper mothering in the sense of love, caring and attention and has consequently developed into an insecure adult lacking in self-esteem, is described as being 'insecurely attached'.

These emotionally deprived people see the world as unsafe and threatening, and when it comes to partner selection, they often choose someone who is 'securely attached', who they assume will nurture them and shield them from the harsh realities of life. In theory this should work well if the securely attached person is able to 'recycle' the love and caring they received as a child. However, insecurely attached individuals often harbour fears that their partner might leave them, which can manifest in self-fulfilling prophecies, whereby they unconsciously behave in a way that drives their partner away.

- Think back to the most recent relationship you had that ended. Make a list of character traits that you found most attractive and least attractive in that person when you first met them.

- Rate those characteristics on a scale of 1–10, with 10 the highest level of attraction.

- Now rate them again as they seemed to you when you broke up.

- What do the differences in ratings tell you about your own needs in a relationship?

Here is the real 'spoiler' that dictates why 'opposites attract' should be amended to read 'like attracts like'. An apparent yawning gulf in personality is often not a gulf at all; in fact the two partners might well be similar deep down. We all manage our anxieties and neuroses in different ways; so, in the example just now, Joe was outwardly self-assured, but he might have been wearing a mask of confidence to cover up feelings of inadequacy and insecurity.

Relationship expert Stephen Betchen, author of *Magnetic Partners*, says that couples who appear to be polar opposites are usually people who have the same 'master conflicts'. By this he means their deepest fear or area of emotional struggle, such as lack of self-esteem or difficulty expressing emotion.

Seeking our twin-in-conflict

In a statement that backs up the unconscious choosing exercise carried out by Robin Skynner at the Institute of Family Therapy, Betchen goes further and claims that if he put someone in a room with 100 people they would choose the one person who has the same underlying conflict.

Betchen states that we unconsciously choose our 'twin-in-conflict' because change is hard and people prefer to stay the same, avoiding the pain involved in changing. By choosing someone who is similar to us on a deeper level, partners can police each other and make sure they remain the same. 'We do not and cannot choose our polar opposites,' he says, 'our subconscious won't allow it.'

Obvious or 'conscious' similarities clearly play a part in attraction, with such things as shared values, religion, cultural background and even hobbies high on the list of relationship drivers. In this context, it is the 'mirror' factor that lies behind these similarities because research has shown that people have an obvious tendency to be drawn into a relationship with people who they recognize as being like them.

A study of almost 1000 residents of New York between the ages of eighteen and 24 asked participants to rate the importance of ten attributes of a long-term partner. They were then made to rate themselves on the same scale. The results revealed that they were far more likely to choose partners who were like themselves in terms of character traits. The attraction of opposites and reproductive potential came out as relatively unimportant.

CASE STUDY Carl and Siobhan had reached the end of the road in their relationship and Siobhan came to see me in what seemed like a token attempt to find some way of patching up their difficulties. They had been married for seven years and had stayed together for the past year or so purely for the sake of their two small children, Amy, aged four, and Thomas, who was two.

The principal source of conflict appeared to revolve around Carl's serial infidelity, although there were yawning gulfs between them on several other major issues. Siobhan had found out about Carl's affair with a female colleague and he had then confessed to several more affairs.

In our early sessions, Siobhan very much played the victim, adopting a 'How could he do this to me?' attitude whilst stressing her own devotion to Carl and painting herself as someone who would never look at another man. When someone overplays a characteristic in themselves it often masks a trait that is completely the opposite, in other words a darker personal quality of which they are ashamed. The term 'reaction formation' is the psychological label used to describe this unconscious denial mechanism.

As the therapy continued and Siobhan became more trusting of me and more willing to open up about herself, she revealed that she had been involved in at least twenty relationships before she met Carl. Most of them were brief and she had never really committed to a man before she got married. She also admitted that she had begun to feel 'caged in' in her marriage fairly early on and was having sexual fantasies about a neighbour, who had made it obvious that he was interested in her.

Although unaware of it, Siobhan had chosen Carl because he shared her 'master conflict' – a fear of intimacy and commitment. Sadly, the wounds from the conflict had cut too deep and they eventually parted. However, Siobhan at least gained insight into the unconscious processes that motivated her when she chose a long-term partner, and she was able to find the roots of her fear of commitment and work on it.

The filter model of partner selection

According to researchers Alan Kerckhoff and Keith Davis, who developed the 'filter' model of relationships, the factors that draw people together go through stages whereby they are gradually 'filtered out'. The Kerckhoff and Davis study, carried out over a seven-month period, compared couples who had been together for less than eighteen months with couples who had been in relationships lasting more than eighteen months.

The basis of the filter model is that potential partners, referred to as the 'field of availables', are narrowed down to a 'field of desirables'. It is from this second group that we choose the person with whom we enter into a relationship. The process involves three stages or 'filters'.

The first filter includes sociological and demographical variables that determine the likelihood of two people meeting in the first place. This throws up a broad sweep of people who are available, and they, in turn, are narrowed down by 'pre-set' factors that they have in common such as race, religion, social class and education. Individual characteristics do not play a part at this stage.

The second filter involves shared attitudes, values, interests and beliefs. This could be described as 'psychological compatibility', although it does not take into account unconscious motivations. The researchers found that the chances of a short-term relationship becoming more permanent depended most on shared beliefs.

Filter number three concerns complementary emotional needs. If a couple have vastly different emotional needs, this does not bode well for the longevity of the relationship, although, as we saw in the chapter on communication, if a couple can at least talk honestly and non-judgementally about their differing needs a compromise can sometimes be reached.

Doorway to a new identity

As we have seen, attraction is multi-layered, but if we take an overview of the psychology of attraction from a more human point of view, what are the over-arching hopes and goals that drive people when they enter a relationship? What do they hope to gain from abandoning the single life and becoming part of a couple?

The clue lies in the words 'becoming part of a couple'. By doing this, people seek to create their own private world, a world that transcends normal life and insulates them from the harsh realities of living. Perhaps this is an unrealistic dream, but it is a very common and understandable one, although the danger of seeking someone to 'complete' or 'fix' us, looked at in Chapter 2, should always be borne in mind.

As well as rising above the ordinariness of day-to-day living, people also seek to transcend themselves. Being in a loving, fulfilling relationship can make us feel special, as well as validated and valued as a human being; and we may even feel 'born again' in the sense that we see ourselves as taking on a new identity. Because of this we often feel empowered to act in new and more daring ways, and to branch out in new directions and take on new challenges.

Entering into a relationship that has long-term potential can also be seen as the start of an exhilarating journey with a caring and empathic companion, who will share the many and varied experiences life has to offer – the joy and the heartache, the passion and the pain. Going through all of this together means that you can develop a deeper understanding, grow together, and, hopefully, grow old together.

A divine accident

Here again the danger of relying on one person to fulfil all your needs cannot be over-emphasized. However, let us end this chapter on a positive note with the following quotation by Sir Hugh Walpole, the celebrated novelist, which sums up these universal aspirations:

The most wonderful of all things in life is the discovery of another human being with whom one's relationship has a growing depth, beauty and joy as the years increase. This inner progressiveness of love between two human beings is a most marvellous thing; it cannot be found by looking for it or by passionately wishing for it. It is a sort of divine accident, and the most wonderful of all things in life.

- When thinking of a long-term relationship, focus on someone who shares the same beliefs and attitudes about the major issues of life.

- Beware of putting too much emphasis on one particular personality trait that seems especially attractive to you in a new partner.

- Bear in mind that someone who seems very different to you might actually be the same underneath.

IF YOU REMEMBER ONE THING

Forget about opposites attracting. That should be applied only to magnetic poles, not viable relationships.

12. Knowing me, knowing you

There's nothing more intimate in life than simply being understood. And understanding someone else.
Brad Meltzer

If you asked a cross-section of people to name the main ingredients for a successful relationship, it is reasonable to assume that intimacy would figure high up on most lists. But what do we really mean by intimacy? For many of us it is a slightly nebulous ideal to which we aspire but which often appears to elude us for a variety of reasons.

There are a thousand different definitions of intimacy and most of them concern the qualities of openness, honesty, and vulnerability, and the willingness to share our deepest fears, desires and other feelings with our partner in order to become closer to them emotionally (the question of sexual intimacy will be dealt with in the next chapter).

This is sometimes described as giving fully of ourselves, or allowing ourselves to be seen as we really are, and thus being fully known in a process of mutual transparency. In her book *The Dance of Intimacy*, Dr Harriet Lerner summarizes an intimate relationship as: 'One in which neither party silences, sacrifices or betrays the self and each party expresses strength and vulnerability, weakness and competence in a balanced way.'

So how do we go about achieving this desired state of mutual sharing, caring and closeness? As I stressed earlier in the book, the starting point for everything in relationships is communication. The more frequent, more honest and more empathic the communication is, the more effective it will be in fostering intimacy.

A major part of that process is a willingness to listen to the other person in a non-judgemental way, giving a full and fair hearing to everything that is being said and, if necessary, agreeing to disagree in an attitude of mutual respect. For respect, we can also use the word 'acceptance', meaning an acknowledgement of the fact that whilst our partner's views, personal attributes and behaviour may be different from ours, that is what makes them who they are.

Peeling back the onion

We live in an age when maintaining an appearance of being cool, in control and 'keeping it together' is regarded as a desirable if not essential state of being. Despite all the moves towards self-reflection and more enlightened human relationships, through psychotherapy, counselling, spirituality, and other routes, the idea of making ourselves vulnerable and showing our weaker, softer side is still unthinkable to many people, in western society at least.

Which brings us to the one vital ingredient I have not mentioned so far: courage – and that is where the principal barrier to intimacy lies. Peeling back the layers of our personal 'onion' can make us feel as if we are being stripped emotionally naked, and that is often too frightening to consider. The underlying fear is usually driven by a belief that if we show ourselves, warts and all, we will be seen as flawed, unworthy, or lacking in some way and will therefore be rejected.

Bill Hybels, author and founder of the influential Willow Creek Association of North American churches, puts it this way: 'For a (marriage) relationship to flourish, there must be intimacy. It takes an enormous amount of courage to say to your spouse, "This is me. I'm not proud of it – in fact, I'm a little embarrassed by it – but this is who I am."'

As mentioned earlier in the book, it is not necessarily a bad thing to keep certain thoughts or feelings from your partner, but when withholding involves issues that directly affect the relationship, or have the potential for doing so, then it is essential to find some way of bringing them into the open. If those things remain unsaid, the difficult feelings can only get worse because they lurk inside like an emotional cancer, and may lead to a build-up of guilt, resentment, frustration and general negativity.

A practical exercise in intimacy

Dr Nathaniel Branden, a respected figure in the field of self-esteem and personal development, and author of *The Psychology of Romantic Love*, uses a fascinating exercise to bring about intimacy between couples who are experiencing stagnation in their relationship or are estranged. The couple must commit to being in the same room alone together for twelve hours, with no distractions whatsoever, including no children, books, television and phone calls.

After an initial awkwardness, irritation and anger often spill out, and resentments, grudges and unhealed wounds are disclosed. This is frequently followed by a softer, more conciliatory phase in which deeper feelings are shared, vulnerabilities revealed and secret longings and dreams disclosed which have previously been off limits. This in turn usually leads to a new sense of closeness through discovery and acceptance of the other person for who they are; although in some cases couples realize that the relationship has run its course and agree to separate.

- Try to think of everything you have ever kept hidden from your current (or previous) partner.

- Divide these things into two categories: those you would be willing to reveal if the circumstances felt right, and those you would never reveal under any circumstances.

- If your partner promised to listen sympathetically and without criticism or judgement in any shape or form, are there any items among the 'prohibited' list that you might consider revealing?

- If he or she promised to reveal some things from their prohibited list, would that encourage you to do the same?

Lack of self-esteem is a major factor when people fear intimacy. If someone harbours deep-seated fears that they are not good enough or inadequate in some way, or that they are seen as unattractive or uninteresting, they will try desperately to cover up that 'unacceptable' side so that others will not be aware of it. This means never allowing anyone to get close enough to see those perceived faults or weaknesses.

Intimacy is unthinkable because it involves openness and disclosure, and that is the very thing that people who are seriously lacking in self-esteem fear most. That does not stop such people forming relationships, but they will nearly always try to keep their partner at a distance in some way and they will often form a 'complementary' partnership with someone who also has a fear of being seen as they really are and of being known fully.

The irony is that people with lack of self-esteem will often compulsively seek relationships in an attempt to get the positive affirmation they need to make them feel 'okay'. However, what they frequently get caught up in when they enter into a relationship is a phenomenon that is sometimes known as 'elastic band syndrome'.

This occurs when they make a conscious attempt to become intimate with the other person but find it impossible to do so. Because their unconscious fears of intimacy are setting the agenda out of their awareness, they reach a point where they find the increasing closeness unbearable and 'ping off' again back to their own private space, where they can remain safe.

Fear as the enemy of intimacy

As mentioned in Chapter 7, in which self-esteem was examined in more detail, people who are severely lacking in this quality often bring about a self-fulfilling prophecy in which they unconsciously 'set-up' the situation they fear. So, for example, someone who believes deep down that they are unattractive, despite everything their partner tells them, might have an overwhelming fear that he or she might leave for someone more attractive.

Because this fear eats away at them, they act in a way that drives the partner away, or into the arms of someone else. This could be brought about in a variety of ways and might involve such things as constantly finding fault with their partner so they eventually find the relationship intolerable, or withholding emotionally and/or sexually so their partner is driven to seek fulfilment elsewhere.

Apart from the fear of being seen as weak or lacking in some way, there are other deep-seated psychological reasons why people fear intimacy and unconsciously avoid it. This fear can manifest itself as an inability to commit to someone, and is often related to an early experience of an overly attentive or intrusive parent, who is seen as being emotionally overwhelming, the classic 'smother mother' type, although fathers can also induce these negative feelings.

Experiences of loss – of a close relative, or a partner, or someone who represented stability and closeness in some form – is another major factor in predisposing an individual to avoiding commitment and intimacy. When individuals suffer a sequence of personal losses they will frequently become 'commitment phobics', avoiding closeness and intimacy all the more because their life script tells them that it is destined to end suddenly or tragically.

A prime characteristic of this phobic attitude in adult love relationships is a tendency to 'dump before you are dumped', in other words to end the relationship as soon as it appears to be going somewhere. This is often an unconscious safety valve for people who have experienced relationship break-ups initiated by the other person because it avoids any possibility of being hurt again.

The 'dump first' scenario featured strongly in the relationship difficulties of a client of mine named Chantal, an attractive woman of French origin, whose adult life was punctuated by a series of short-lived relationships. Chantal's father had left when she was four and her mother died when she was eight. She had then been brought up by an aunt, who passed away suddenly when Chantal was fifteen. Furthermore, her first 'serious' boyfriend, who she met at university when she was eighteen, had left her for someone else just when she was becoming emotionally attached to him.

This sequence of losses made it glaringly obvious why Chantal would want to avoid getting close to anyone, but, despite all my efforts, she refused to acknowledge what was really going on, namely that she was always the one to end the fledgling relationship as soon as her partner began to show signs of wanting to take their association to a deeper and more committed level. She invariably put it down to something *they* had done.

The breakthrough came after she had been seeing me for about six months. She arrived one day looking particularly anxious and informed me that she wanted to end therapy immediately. When I asked her why she had decided to finish, she said that it was because of money being tight, which I knew could not be true because she earned a very good salary as an executive in television.

Halfway through the session she became visibly agitated and asked me if I would mind if she left early. Suddenly it hit me: Chantal's decision to leave therapy so suddenly was another example of her acting out her greatest fear. Our relationship, albeit professional, was by its very nature becoming closer and more intimate over time, so she had decided to cut me off before I could do it to her.

When I put this suggestion to Chantal, she became extremely emotional and eventually admitted that she had been afraid of becoming too close to me and felt her only option was to end therapy before I found a reason to end it with her. This episode proved transformative. Chantal was able to work on her deep-seated fear and, by allowing herself to stay on with me in therapy, she was able to see that her script could be changed; that getting close to someone did not necessarily mean they would abandon her.

Different routes to intimacy?

Dr Harriet Lerner, whose summary of an intimate relationship was given earlier, highlights what she regards as a major difference between the sexes when it comes to fostering intimacy in a relationship. She writes: 'Men often feel at a loss about how to become experts on close relationships, although their anxiety may be masked by apathy or disinterest.

'Many men have been raised by fathers who were most conspicuous by their emotional or physical absence and omnipresent mothers whose very "feminine" qualities and traits they, as males, were taught to repudiate in themselves … Men tend to distance from a partner (or get a new one) when the going gets rough, rather than hang in and struggle for change.'

There is a degree of truth in the suggestion that men and women can have different ways of achieving closeness and dealing with conflict, but Lerner's comments constitute another generalization which simply perpetuates the stereotyping of men and woman and the 'unbridgeable divide' between them. Women also tend to suffer emotional fallout from absent fathers, equally so in my experience. Furthermore, it is clearly not just men who tend to seek new partners when the going gets rough because some 70 per cent of divorces are initiated by women in the UK, a figure that is mirrored in the USA.

In my view, men and women can struggle equally to bring about genuine, meaningful closeness, and if people carry around the idea that there are different routes to intimacy for the sexes it creates an artificial and unnecessary barrier between them. For both sexes, the only way to overcome difficulties in achieving a truly intimate relationship is through communication, and understanding and acceptance of your partner's 'barriers to intimacy'.

Importance of knowing yourself

What is often overlooked, however, is the fact that it is equally important to achieve understanding and acceptance of yourself. If you are suffering from emotional fallout from past experiences and have never genuinely attempted to heal those old wounds – whether it is through psychotherapy, counselling, or any other form of meaningful self-reflection – this will invariably affect your ability to achieve intimacy.

You will carry this emotional baggage into any new relationship and because it has not been dealt with effectively it will cause you to build defensive barriers between yourself and your partner. For example, if you have a 'sensitive area' based on an earlier experience of loss or rejection that you keep hidden away, you might constantly be hypervigilant for signs that it could be repeated; or you might become angry, uncommunicative or sulky if your partner unintentionally touches on this issue.

So, when you are in an ongoing relationship, it is always important to be fully aware of your weak spots and to notice when they become a hindrance to open communication or a source of conflict. Fear of something is usually worse than the thing itself; working on that fear and eventually bringing it out into the open is the only way to move forward.

- Remember that whilst intimacy is one word it is certainly not one-dimensional. True intimacy covers many areas and issues in a relationship.

- The title of this chapter, 'Knowing me, knowing you', should serve as a watchword for achieving intimacy in relationships.

- Factor in some 'honesty time' in your week when you and your partner agree to reveal at least one secret fear or anxiety.

- Make a conscious effort to discover and admit your own fears, anxieties and difficult feelings and work on them, with professional help if necessary.

 Intimacy does not just happen. Like so many other ingredients for successful relationships, it needs to be worked on constantly and never taken for granted.

---

13. The myth of sex

*Love is the answer, but while you are waiting for
the answer, sex raises some pretty good questions.*
Woody Allen

It might seem surprising that I have positioned the chapter on sex nearer the end of the book than the beginning. This was a deliberate strategy designed to illustrate that we as a society place too much emphasis on sex and the relentless pursuit of sexual pleasure as a kind of recreational 'must have' and a pre-condition to successful relationships.

Because of the way sex has been overplayed and devalued in films, books, newspapers and the media generally, it has lost much of its specialness, exclusivity and, to a great extent, its meaning. Sex should be a source of pleasure, joy and intimacy between two people, a natural enhancer of relationships. However, performance and evaluation have, for many people, become more important than mutual enjoyment and shared experience.

We now speak about someone being 'good in bed' as if there is some kind of universal standard by which we must all be measured when we slip between the sheets. We also talk of having a 'sex life', as if that part of us is somehow divorced from the rest of our being, especially the psychological and emotional parts, which of course it is not. As has often been said – and equally often ignored – the principal erogenous zone of the body is the mind.

Another common misconception

Sigmund Freud's theory of human sexuality is frequently misrepresented, especially his use of the term 'libido', which, in current usage, has come to mean someone's sex drive. Freud used 'libido' to denote a form of mental energy, which he originally saw as being solely attached to our sexual instincts. However, he later came to regard libido as a form of mental or 'psychic' energy that was part of the broader 'life force' or 'life instinct' in human beings; so the popular idea that Freud saw sex as being at the basis of all human activity is understandable but not wholly accurate.

Freud went on to suggest that the way in which our libido is expressed depends upon the stage of psychological development we have reached; and he said that children develop through a series of 'psychosexual stages' (such as the oral, anal and phallic stages) in which the libido is focused on a specific area. If each stage is successfully negotiated, the child will move on to the next stage of development and this will enable them to reach a healthy state of adulthood.

Unrealistic expectations

There is no doubt that the over-emphasis on sex has impacted relationships in a negative way by creating unrealistic expectations. People have been conditioned to expect a 'good sex life' as a major component of a success- ful ongoing relationship. Furthermore, there is a growing belief that the standard of sexual harmony and fulfilment must never be allowed to drop regardless of what else is going on within the relationship.

The level of false expectation does not stop there. We have bought into several great lies about sex, including the idea that there is an optimum number of times couples should have sex, and for women that there is a prescribed number of orgasms they should have during sex. The great deception for men is that they must be 'superstuds', ready, willing and able at all times to provide complete sexual satisfaction for their partners.

There is also the myth of simultaneous orgasms being the desired high point for sexual fulfillment, which puts yet another pressure on couples to conform to impossible standards. Sex should be about closeness and joy and above all *humanity*, not robotic achievement, which is why I believe we should treat these false messages with the traditional pinch of salt and take note of another quote from Woody Allen, who said: 'The only time my wife and I had a simultaneous orgasm was when the judge signed the divorce papers'.

Not only are these 'performance myths' misguided, they are also dangerous. It is simply not possible for sex between two people in a long-term partnership to remain at the same level throughout. Inevitably there will be peaks and troughs, depending on factors such as the more general state of the relationship; each partner's personal circumstances, including their health and emotional well-being; major life events such as family bereavements, job losses, and the birth of children; and physical changes brought about by advancing years.

It is also important to remember that people are individuals and have different levels of sexual need or desire, which in turn can vary over time. People do not conform to some universal sexual template, so it is crucial to accept your partner's sexual needs and not expect them necessarily to match your own.

Compromise and understanding is the name of the game, as it is in so many other areas of relationships. Failure to accept differences and work on a suitable way of bridging the divide will only result in resentment and conflict.

Sex not a crucial factor

Research by Charles and Elizabeth Schmitz, authors of *Building a Love That Lasts*, has shown that sex is relatively low on the list of factors contributing to lasting and harmonious relationships.

Couples were asked to rate how important sex was in the success of their marriage on a scale of 1–10, with 10 being the highest. Over a 27-year period, the average rating was only 6. The conclusion from the two researchers was: 'No marriage was ever saved or made successful because the couple had a great sex life!'

TRY IT NOW!

- On a scale of 1–10, rate how important sex is in a relationship in general terms.

- Do you sometimes feel under unspoken pressure to have sex in your current relationship.

- Do you feel you have to reach certain standards in bed to make sex 'good'?

- How crucial is the maintenance of 'good sex' in your current relationship?

In the final analysis, sex is one of many factors that affect the success of relationships. However, we must be careful not to go down the route of the singer Boy George, who famously said: 'I would rather have a cup of tea than sex', because whilst this often infuriating and frustrating three-letter word can assume a position of undue importance, it should be an integral and enriching ingredient of most relationships.

I have used the word 'most' because there are certain qualifications to that last statement. For example, some couples, particularly those in their more mature years, agree to have platonic, or non-sexual relationships and this can work very well. The key here is that they have *agreed* about the 'no sex' format of their relationship because, as with every other component of relationships – and I make no apology for emphasizing this point again – communication is the key.

All in the mind

In pursuing this theme, let us look first at the belief that sex should take place on a regular basis and be of a consistently high quality. As mentioned earlier, the vital factor that so often gets overlooked or dismissed is that sex is far more about what goes on between the ears than between the legs.

Sex is a basic urge and need, not just for the purpose of having children, but because it gives pleasure on more than one level and is a way of creating intimacy and bonding between two people. However, in order to feel like having sex, an individual has to be mentally as well as physically 'up for it'; and if he or she is not in the right frame of mind, which can happen for a variety of reasons, their sexual functioning on a physical level will be impaired, or it may not happen at all.

So, for example, if a man comes home from work feeling in the mood for sex and tries to sweet-talk his wife into bed, he should not be surprised or disappointed if, after a demanding day with their two young children and a host of un-stimulating domestic chores, she is not particularly responsive (although this can sometimes be an indicator of a deeper problem that is not being talked about). Or if a woman feels like making love and her partner has been under pressure at work, she should not expect fireworks in the bedroom.

When sex becomes another pressure

Taking a longer term perspective, someone who is depressed or stressed, or deeply unhappy for whatever reason, may well regard sex as just another pressure they can do without and may even lose their sex drive altogether. This is when the need for meaningful communication becomes essential.

People often feel rejected when their partner does not want to make love; and this can become a serious issue if the partner loses interest in sex altogether. Not talking about it will only increase resentment and negative thinking, or may even lead them to suspect that their partner is having an affair.

When a couple are in the middle of a period of rowing this is usually a 'killer' as far as sex is concerned. However, some couples use fighting as a way of re-energizing their relationship and for them a blazing row can often be a precursor to passionate sex.

In today's high-speed world, finding time for sex can often be difficult, so it is frequently overlooked by default. Once again, it is vital to talk to your partner if you feel the sexual side of your relationship is not how you would like it to be.

Despite our more open and supposedly enlightened attitude to sex, it is still in some ways one of the last great taboos. People fear talking about worries or difficulties connected with sex because they fear being seen as inadequate or deficient in some way. And the messages we receive from all around us telling us that we must be up to standard in the bedroom feed into this.

Sex is great when it works well, but it can put huge pressure on people when they feel they have failed in some way, a remark that applies equally to men and women. If it can be spoken about honestly and freely, without judgement or any sense of attack or criticism, it can be one of the best ways of creating genuine intimacy and closeness.

Sex as a form of communication

Whilst communication between partners *about* sex is a must, it must not be forgotten that sex is in itself a form of communication. When we have sex we are seeking physical pleasure and release, but we are also searching for connection, love and transcendence, and we are expressing who we are.

One of most powerful, motivational facets of human nature is that people are crying out to be known, to be accepted, to be made to feel special and, through these affirmations, to love themselves. Having sex is a way of saying 'Understand me', 'Like me', 'Love me'. Even in the most transient sexual encounters there is always an element of psychological need or craving underlying the physical desire.

So the classic Casanova or Don Juan is almost invariably using sex as a way of shoring up a fragile ego. It is the same with the female equivalent, nymphomania, which the *Oxford English Dictionary* describes as 'uncontrollable or excessive sexual desire in women'. For the nymphomaniac herself the word 'excessive' has a darker connotation; it signifies an interminable quest for something that is missing in terms of her ability to find satisfaction, not sexually but emotionally.

The irony of these brief liaisons is that they bring nothing but emptiness and sometimes self-loathing, which is the opposite of what the Casanova or the nymphomaniac craves. Hence the need always to be moving on to the next conquest or casual encounter in search of the real prize – respect, acceptance and love.

In today's sex-obsessed society there is also a general feeling that we must not hold back in terms of having multiple partners; in fact, for many people it is considered old-fashioned or un-cool to be discriminating in the selection and number of your sexual partners.

Furthermore, the idea of preserving one's virginity until marriage is widely regarded as a matter for ridicule rather than admiration, which is not only a cynical comment on the personal values of our times, but also feeds into the 'If it feels good do it' mentality that has trivialized sex in such a damaging way.

Elsa came to see me because she was desperately unhappy in her relationship. One of the primary causes of her unhappiness was her husband's demands for what she referred to as 'kinky' sex. This mostly consisted of role-playing in which he would get her to dress up in various uniforms, but occasionally there was a degree of sadomasochism (the infliction and/or receiving of pain) as well.

Elsa told me that these 'sex games' made her feel humiliated and 'dirty', and to add to her feelings of extreme discomfort, her husband sneered at her unresponsiveness, making her feel that there was something wrong with her because she was not totally uninhibited. Because of his constant belittling of her, Elsa came to believe that she *was* at fault and told me that she felt her inexperience – she had been involved in 'only three previous sexual relationships' to use her words – was a factor.

Her husband became angry when Elsa suggested marriage counselling and refused even to contemplate it. After a series of sessions with me it became obvious that the only way forward as far as Elsa was concerned was to leave him, which she was understandably reluctant to do because of their two young children.

Elsa's situation was a classic example of one person failing totally to accept that their partner's sexual needs were different from theirs. Furthermore, her belief that she was inexperienced and inadequate highlighted the current vogue for over-emphasizing standards of sexual performance at the expense of caring and sharing, and mutual understanding and compromise.

Differing approaches to sex

In previous chapters, I have been keen to stress the dangers of over-emphasizing gender differences with regard to various relationship issues. However, there are some fundamental distinctions in the way men and women approach sex. As a broad generalization, the old adage which says: 'Men seek love through sex and women seek sex through love' has a degree of truth in it.

A major survey of sexual practices in the USA, led by Dr Edward O. Laumann, of the University of Chicago, reached the conclusion that sexual desire in women is extremely sensitive to environment and context, whereas men's sexual drives are generally stronger and more straightforward.

The study also found that men think more about sex and seek sex more avidly; that is to say, they want it more throughout a long-term relationship, and they also seek more sexual relationships and casual sex than women. Men are also more visual when it comes to arousal. Women take a 'less direct' route to sexual satisfaction, i.e. more situational and connected to their emotions.

Once again we must be careful of stereotyping because context and emotions do affect men's sexuality, albeit in a less obvious way, and not all men are serial womanizers. And women can be just as instantly turned on by sexual images and fantasies, and they can and do indulge in casual sex, increasingly so in these days of ever greater sexual freedom. Both sexes can be equally prone to infidelity, as we shall see in the next chapter.

- Remember that sex does not only involve communication, it is also *about* communication.

- Accept that there will always be differences in people's sex drives, both in the long and short term.

- Sex should be about caring and sharing, not performance and standards.

Be careful not to put an over-emphasis on sex. Try to see it as one valuable aspect of your relationship and one of several paths to intimacy.

14. Forsaking all others?

*There lives within the very flame of love a kind of wick
or snuff that will abate it*
William Shakespeare

If there is one relationship issue that stirs up interest even more than sex it is infidelity. There is a considerable divergence of views on whether it is natural, unavoidable, whether men are more prone to it than women, and how to deal with it when it happens. And if you are looking for factual evidence, there are statistics to indicate patterns and trends as to who does what with whom and how often, but research in this area is by no means conclusive, especially when it comes to the big question: 'Why?'

Having said that, our view of infidelity appears to be consistent in one respect. The British Social Attitudes Survey reveals that despite the apparent ethos of greater sexual freedom in our society, opinion about extra-marital sex has remained constant over two decades, with over 60 per cent of the population believing it is always wrong.

Research also shows that some 90 per cent of newly married women and over 80 per cent of newly married men say that they intend to remain sexually faithful. However, to quote the character Azeem in *Robin Hood: Prince of Thieves* 'There are no perfect men in the world; only perfect intentions.' Those words highlight the underlying psychology of infidelity: we might intend to remain faithful to our partners, but there are many factors luring us, urging us, or even predisposing us to do the opposite.

Emotional-physical split

Intriguingly, whilst men have traditionally been seen as more likely to stray, research indicates that there is not a huge gap between the sexes in this respect. A study in the US-based *Journal of Couple and Relationship Therapy* revealed that around 60 per cent of men and 50 per cent of women will have an extramarital affair at some stage during their relationship.

Before we delve deeper into what drives people to be unfaithful, it is important to define what we mean by infidelity. For most people, it would constitute your partner having sex with someone else. However, having been at pains throughout the book to sound a note of caution regarding a fixed view of gender differences, there does appear to be a disparity between men and women in terms of how they regard infidelity and what constitutes being unfaithful.

Men are usually hurt far more by the physical aspect when their partner has an affair, whilst women generally find the emotional betrayal hardest to deal with. This is reflected in the fact that men are more likely to cite adultery as grounds for divorce than women.

For women, it is the idea of their partner's emotional intimacy with someone else that often matters more than the sexual element; whereas for men, the physical act of betrayal by their partner is connected to their view of what it means to be a man, which in turn is driven by their instinctive rivalry with other men.

 Angela came to see me for general feelings of anxiety and depression; it soon became clear, however, that her empty, unaffectionate relationship of 15 years was the major cause of her unhappiness. Angela told me that she and her husband, Callum, had not made love for over a year, and that he always found some excuse to avoid sex.

Callum had been returning home increasingly late from work and, under pressure from Angela, he confessed that he had become close to one of his female colleagues, who he described as stimulating and witty company. They shared a mutual love of modern art and had been to several exhibitions together, as well as visiting galleries in London, close to where they worked.

'I've asked him outright on several occasions if he's been sleeping with her,' Angela told me. 'And every time he's been adamant that they're just good friends and there's nothing physical between them. He even said that he doesn't fancy her in that way at all, and I believe him because I can always tell when Callum's lying.

'To tell you the truth, though' she added, 'I'd rather their relationship was about sex because I could deal with that.

Knowing that he's getting so close to her in that "meeting of minds" kind of way is far more hurtful to me than if he was just screwing her.'

Evolutionary basis for mate-guarding

As mentioned in Chapter 4, there is an anthropological basis for the differing attitudes of the sexes, which is summarized by Dr Helen Fisher in her book *Why We Love*: 'Because possessiveness is so common in nature, animal behaviourists have given it a name: mate guarding … Generally it is the male who guards the female – from poachers, and from defection by the female. For sound evolutionary reasons. If a male can sequester a female during her ovulation, she may bear his offspring and pass his genes towards eternity.'

The payoff for women is small compared to men in terms of reproductive benefits. Unlike men they cannot engage in multiple fertilizations and, furthermore, they can only get pregnant during certain periods of their menstrual cycle. These basic differences in the capacity for child production have led to the suggestion that it is not natural for women to stray because there is no biological purpose.

Fisher disputes this, offering four reasons why adultery could have been biologically adaptive for our female ancestors. First, a diversity of male partners could provide a woman with a variety of practical and material benefits for her and her offspring; second, adultery was a form of insurance in case a woman's primary partner died or left; third, if a woman had a partner who was defective physically or emotionally, she could 'upgrade' her genetic line by having children by a more viable male; fourth, having children with a variety of partners, increased the likelihood that some of them would survive fluctuations in the environment.

A myth about female sexuality

The widely held belief that men are more likely to stray because by nature they are more 'into' casual encounters does not hold water. One of the conclusions of the famous and controversial *Kinsey Report*, which was in fact two reports, one into male sexual behaviour (1948) and another into female sexual behaviour (1953), was: 'Even in those cultures which most rigorously attempt to control the female's extramarital coitus, it is perfectly clear that such activity does occur, and in many instances it occurs with considerable regularity.'

In their book, *Why Women Have Sex*, psychologists Cindy Meston and David Buss debunk the idea that women do it for love and men for pleasure. The main reason women have sex, they discovered, is pure physical enjoyment: orgasms, and plenty of them.

In all, Meston and Buss came up with 237 reasons why women have sex, which, apart from basic biological drives, included promotion, money, drugs, revenge and many diverse and unconnected motives. The second most important reason, by the way, was romantic love.

However, Helen Daly, deputy editor of *Cosmopolitan* magazine, which is renowned for promoting female sexual liberation, provided a surprisingly contrasting view by stating that there is a difference between men and women in their attitudes to casual, or 'no strings' sex.

Highlighting a survey in *Cosmopolitan* which revealed that whilst 64 per cent of women thought it was possible to have no strings sex, only 17 per cent said they actually preferred it, compared to 44 per cent of men, Daly said: 'We've come a long way towards female empowerment in the bedroom, but our greater emotional engagement can still make sexual relationships a conundrum for us.'

- Make a 'sun' diagram with the word 'infidelity' written in a circle. The 'rays' which radiate out from it should be words or phrases that you automatically connect with infidelity, such as 'betrayal', 'loss of trust', 'hurt'.

- Which of these factors would most affect you if your partner had an affair?

- Do you regard infidelity as always unforgivable and an automatic reason for the relationship to end?

In psychological terms, infidelity is a multi-layered phenomenon and rarely just about a physical act. Being unfaithful to your partner can often represent a statement that is consciously or unconsciously meant to draw attention to more general deficiencies in the relationship, for example: 'You don't pay me any attention, so I've found someone who will', or 'I'm looking for someone to make me feel desirable and special because you just take me for granted.'

People often have affairs even though they are in a relatively healthy relationship because they feel the need for reassurance that they are desirable and attractive. This can be heightened as the years pass and the physical side of the relationship inevitably loses its original passion.

Effect of low self-esteem

The need for validation will be especially strong if an individual lacks self-esteem. Such a person may sabotage perfectly healthy relationships if they need constant reassurance, and in some cases, where self-esteem is extremely poor, no amount of reassurance will be enough, so they stumble from one person to another in a never-ending quest to feel 'okay'.

If someone feels deep down that they are unlovable and do not deserve a loving relationship they might also unconsciously engineer things so that their partner is driven to have an affair. This kind of self-fulfilling prophecy, mentioned earlier in the book, confirms their belief that being abandoned and rejected was destined to happen to them. A history of personal losses, such as the deaths of close relatives, or previous relationship break-ups, can be a trigger for this form of self-sabotage.

Sometimes people are attracted by the sheer novelty of an affair. A quick fling can make people feel special because they experience an aliveness that has been lost in the current relationship. The sense of rekindled passion can be reinforced by their new partner seeing them as exciting and new, without the burden of day-to-day domesticity.

Human beings have an innate streak of self-destructiveness and there are times when temptation is simply too much to resist, especially if our ongoing relationship has begun to lose its lustre; common sense and moral sense can be thrown away and we simply go for it without thinking of the consequences. This can be a particularly powerful motivating factor if an individual has little experience of previous relationships and feels they have missed out.

Freud's concept of the Oedipus complex

When a partner has an affair the trust between a couple, which might have seemed impregnable, is shattered and the sense of shock heightens the feeling of betrayal. The reason why people feel so hurt can also be attributed to the element of secrecy, which provides much of the motivation and spice for affairs, and to the fact that there is suddenly a 'triangular' nature to the relationship; in other words, it is no longer an exclusive partnership because it now involves three people.

One of Freud's most famous concepts, the 'Oedipus complex', often underpins these feelings which arise as a result of a secret affair coming to light; that is to say, suddenly finding yourself involved in a three-sided relationship in which you are the one who is shut out. In basic terms, the Oedipus complex refers to feelings connected to a child's wish to possess the parent of the opposite sex and eliminate that of the same sex. The complex took its name from the myth of Oedipus, who killed his father and married his mother without knowing that they were his parents.

The dynamics of the Oedipus complex are often played out in triangular family situations (they are usually confined to psychological interaction between family members and are not acted out, as such). For example, if a father appears to be paying his daughter too much attention and she responds by playing up the 'Daddy's gorgeous little girl' routine, her mother might feel shut out and back off from him sexually; and she might also take out her feelings of jealousy on the daughter.

When a partner has an affair, it can revive memories of this type of Oedipal situation; so if the one who has been betrayed experienced similar feelings in childhood, the infidelity will feel even more hurtful.

Should relationships last 'for life'?

When considering the nature and impact of infidelity, we must always remember that humans are by nature sexual beings and do not stop looking at and fantasizing about other people when they are involved in ongoing, healthy relationships. To do so is perfectly natural; it is when attraction and fantasy become something more that problems start. The big question here is: should we regard it as natural or viable that relationships should be regarded as being permanent or 'for life'?

The Western idea of marriage as an exclusive partnership between two people is seen in perspective when we take into consideration the fact that some 80 per cent of societies allow polygamous marriage. Furthermore, anthropologists have shown that monogamy is not a fixed and natural state for humans.

Helen Fisher puts it this way: 'It seems to be the destiny of humankind that we are neurologically able to love more than one person at a time. You can feel profound attachment for a long-term spouse, while you feel romantic passion for someone in the office or your social circle, while you feel the sex drive as you read a book, watch a movie, or do something else unrelated to your partner.'

If it is true that human beings are programmed to cheat on their mates they are in good company. Of the 4000 species of mammals on this planet only a handful are known to be monogamous. Fidelity is literally for the birds because, by contrast, some 92 per cent of the 9,700 bird species find a mate and stick with them through rain and shine.

Impact of increased lifespans

A major change in our world that is taking place right now needs mentioning in this context. Increased lifespans have added weight to the argument that it is unrealistic to expect one person to fulfil an individual's needs for the entire period of the relationship. Those who promote this viewpoint usually highlight the impossibility of one person being able to satisfy their partner's sexual needs indefinitely.

This argument could be extended to every aspect of human need within the context of relationships, whether it is psychological, emotional, practical, or a combination of all these. In this context, the old cliché 'The grass is always greener on the other side of the fence' should come to mind because the attraction of an affair usually promises more than it delivers.

People often regret ending a long-term relationship for something which seemed to offer more excitement but eventually proves to lack the deeper qualities of the original relationship; which is why it is vital to keep your partner's good points in mind when the relationship is going through a rough patch.

No one can offer support, care and understanding 100 per cent of the time; it is simply not humanly possible. Furthermore, we are constantly changing and – hopefully – maturing as the years pass, so our attitudes to our partners cannot possibly remain constant for the long haul.

However, these changes do not mean that the relationship must, of necessity, be damaged in some way; indeed a relationship can be enhanced by positive changes in one or both partners, especially if the biggest word of all 'communication' is fully respected. And change that is dealt with positively can lead to new ways of relating, often on a deeper, more meaningful level.

- Remember that it is natural to continue finding other people attractive when you are in a relationship. It is when it becomes more than just a fantasy that it is cause for concern.

- If your partner has an affair, or is more than usually attracted to someone else, it can usually be related to wider issues connected to the overall state of your relationship.

- If you are tempted to 'play away', always ask yourself 'Why?' Is it because you are feeling neglected or taken for granted? If so, talk about it!

When you are fed up or bored with your relationship and the lure of an attractive 'outsider' seems irresistible, always take time to pause and think. Try to focus on the positive features of your current partner. Don't throw a good thing away!

---

15. The mystery of love

*Love isn't finding a perfect person. It's seeing an
imperfect person perfectly.*
Sam Keen

So far we have looked at some of the crucial 'make or break'
factors affecting relationships, such as communication,
change, intimacy, conflict and sex. For many people, however, there is an assumption that these matters will fall into
place naturally if a partnership has what is widely regarded
as the essential glue that binds a couple together – love.

This assumption about love is often linked to a pre-
sumption that it is something that happens automatically
when two people meet who are right for one another on
a fundamental level. This is frequently accompanied by a
belief that there is one person out there who is your missing
or complementary 'other half'; a notion fuelled by romantic
movies, novels and songs.

As I highlighted in Chapter 2, the idea of finding one's
other half or 'the one' is as dangerous as it is misleading.
Only you can complete yourself; relying on someone else
to do that for you will inevitably result in disappointment
because no one, no matter how caring and empathic they
might be, can be expected to fulfil their partner's needs
totally, provide unwavering support and understanding,

and fill the emotional void which many people carry inside them.

Any expectations on that level should be the first thing to be discarded when entering a relationship. So, if that is the case, what should we be looking for when we aspire to a relationship based on love? Is love an elusive, mystical experience that is given to only a select group of fortunate individuals, or can it be accessed by anyone who is willing to make an effort?

More importantly, should we align ourselves with the overarching message of The Beatles song *All You Need is Love*? In other words, does love 'fix' everything? To answer those questions we must first decide what it is that we mean by love, a complex undertaking that has challenged, inspired and divided men and women throughout the ages.

Categories of love

In Tolstoy's epic novel *Anna Karenina*, the heroine Anna is challenged for her definition of love during a light-hearted discussion on the subject at an elite social gathering. She responds with the following: 'If it is true that there are as many minds as there are heads, then there are as many kinds of love as there are hearts.'

Anna's words highlight a basic truth: to a greater or lesser extent, we all love in different ways. Any attempt to provide a catch-all definition tends to detract from the dimension of subjective experience, which is arguably the most important factor of all. And, in the final analysis, love is just a word; it can have any meaning we attribute to it.

The Greeks had names for six different types of love – *storge* (friendly), *agape* (unselfish), *mania* (possessive), *pragma* (practical), *lodus* (playful) and *eros* (lustful).

In his book, *The Act of Will*, Roberto Assagioli, a former disciple of Freud and the founder of the psychosynthesis approach to psychotherapy, categorizes love as follows: self love, maternal and paternal love, love between a man and a woman, passionate love, sentimental love, idealistic love, fraternal love, altruistic and humanitarian love, impersonal love, idolatrous love, and the love of God.

For the purposes of this book, I will focus on Assagioli's third category – love between men and women (though I would include same-sex love in this category). As we shall see, it contains aspects of some of the other categories listed above. As Anna Karenina suggested, however, you would need to speak to everyone who has ever loved to provide a truly comprehensive definition that does justice to the complexity and the eternal mystery of love.

For this reason I will not attempt to offer an absolute definition of love, but rather a kind of broad-brush picture. As a taster, I have provided below some thought-provoking attempts to define this most complicated, multifaceted, unfathomable, and frequently infuriating four-letter word, focusing on genuine, lasting love rather than the idealized Hollywood version. The first, from Sir Hugh Walpole, was used in an earlier chapter, but it is worth repeating in this context.

Quotations about love

The most wonderful of all things in life is the discovery of another human being with whom one's relationship has a growing depth, beauty and joy as the years increase. This inner progressiveness of love between two human beings is a most marvellous thing; it cannot be found by looking for it or by passionately wishing for it. It is a sort of divine accident, and the most wonderful of all things in life.

Sir Hugh Walpole

Love means to commit oneself without guarantee, to give oneself completely in the hope that our love will produce love in the loved person. Love is an act of faith, and whoever is of little faith is also of little love.

Erich Fromm

Love is like a friendship caught on fire: in the beginning a flame, very pretty, often hot and fierce, but still only light and flickering. As love grows older, our hearts mature and our love becomes as coals, deep-burning and unquenchable.

Bruce Lee

In real love you want the other person's good. In romantic love you want the other person.

Margaret Anderson

*Love seems the swiftest, but it is the slowest of all growths.
No man or woman really knows what perfect love is until
they have been married a quarter of a century.*

Mark Twain

The first duty of love is to listen.

Paul Tillich

*The will to extend one's self for the purpose of nurturing
one's own or another's spiritual growth.*

Scott Peck

- List the essential qualities of love as you see them.

- Divide these into 'non-negotiable' and 'desirable'.

- Do you believe that love just happens, or does it take time and effort?

- Is love the essential 'glue' in a relationship?

Many of the qualities contained in that list of quotations should be considered givens in any list of ingredients for genuine love. I do not claim that my own definition is comprehensive, or that it is 'the truth'. My hope is that by teasing out and examining some vital components that characterize genuine love between non-related adults, I will be able to offer a set of guidelines for making and keeping happier, healthier, more durable relationships.

My own version is as follows:

Love that is meaningful and enduring requires that two people reach a level of affection, commitment, and regard for the other's welfare that transcends self-serving needs and desires and looks instead to the nurture, support and growth of the other person and the relationship itself. This will usually take time to develop fully and it includes an essential element of not giving up on that relationship when things begin to go wrong.

On the contrary, it means working through the difficulties, being as open and honest as possible, and not needing to win arguments or insisting 'I am right'. Perhaps more important than anything else, it involves those three crucial factors I have stressed throughout this book – communication, communication, communication. It also means wanting the best for each other in terms of personal development and fulfilment and helping your partner to achieve that.

Love at first sight

If my definition sounds somewhat prosaic compared to more idealized depictions of romantic love that is not a bad thing, because the first thing that must be acknowledged is that love does not just happen. The notion of love at first sight is a fantasy for the simple reason that you cannot love someone you do not know.

As revealed earlier in the book, there are complex psychological and biochemical drivers at work when we feel instantly drawn to someone we have never met before. These powerful feelings – often referred to as 'chemistry' – may eventually become love, but they do not constitute love in their initial 'raw' state.

In Sir Hugh Walpole's definition, he talks of love as being a 'divine accident'; the idea of it being something that is preordained or 'meant to happen' is qualified by highlighting its progressive nature. It is human nature to aspire to the romantic ideals of one special person with whom you make an instant connection but, like so many other worthwhile things in life, a lasting, loving relationship needs to be carefully constructed and worked at continually.

Learning the art of love

In *The Art of Loving*, Erich Fromm says that love is an art just as living is an art: 'If we want to learn how to love we must proceed in the same way we have to proceed if we want to learn any other art, say music, painting, carpentry, or the art of medicine or engineering.' He goes on to say that the process of learning an art, in this case love, can be divided into theory and practice; that these two must be blended in order to master the art.

Fromm claims that people rarely try to learn the art of love because: 'In spite of the deep-seated craving for love, almost everything else is considered to be more important than love: success, prestige, money, power.' I would go along with that last statement in as much as many people feel that they do not need to invest time and energy into making love into a real and lasting thing. They have an expectation that being with the 'right' person will automatically make this happen.

Sternberg's triangular theory

Psychologist Robert Sternberg formulated the 'triangular' theory of love, which stipulated three components – intimacy, passion and commitment. Sternberg maintained that various combinations of these three components produce different kinds of love; for example romantic love is characterized by intimacy and passion, companionate love is based on intimacy and commitment, and infatuated love on passion alone.

The complete and ideal form of love is 'consummate love' (see the diagram opposite), which has intimacy, passion and commitment. However, Sternberg's thinking is very much in line with Fromm's 'practice makes perfect' approach, as he warns that once it is achieved consummate love needs to be worked at and cannot be guaranteed to last forever without effort and will.

In *The Transformation of Intimacy*, Anthony Giddens uses the term 'confluent love' to describe a situation between two people which 'presumes equality in emotional give and take'. He suggests that love 'only develops to the degree to which intimacy does, to the degree to which each partner is prepared to reveal concerns and

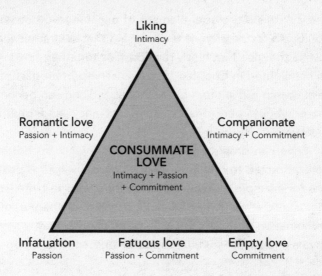

Liking
Intimacy

Romantic love
Passion + Intimacy

Companionate
Intimacy + Commitment

CONSUMMATE LOVE
Intimacy + Passion + Commitment

Infatuation
Passion

Fatuous love
Passion + Commitment

Empty love
Commitment

needs to the other and to be vulnerable to that other'. This is an admirable summary of the importance of genuine intimacy for a lasting and mutually fulfilling love relationship.

As a more succinct definition of what constitutes an enduring, loving relationship, it would be difficult to better the expression used by Harville Hendrix in *Getting The Love You Want*, in which he describes how he and his wife have arrived at a stage which he terms 'passionate friendship'. Friendship is so often cited as the basis for a lasting love relationship that it is almost a cliché, but it is no less valid for that.

An essential element of true friendship is that we respect the other person for who they are and accept them 'warts and all'; this is a crucial element of genuine love between adults. As for passion, it is often said that sex rather than love is the glue that holds relationships together; however as highlighted in Chapter 13, sex is an important part of a relationship but is often over-emphasized and can become more about performance than intimacy and mutual pleasure.

Love can grow between two people who are not initially attracted to one another in a physical way. It is possible, for example, to have a passion for someone's intellect, their sense of humour, or their kind, charitable nature, or a combination of those things. To put it another way, we can have a passion for someone's soul or their spiritual essence.

The element of togetherness

Togetherness is often cited as a key principle of a loving relationship, but that is a rather nebulous concept, and too often couples fall into a 'living in each other's pockets' way of relating that is more about possession and ownership than a healthy closeness. Retaining one's identity and a degree of separateness does not preclude togetherness, which is an altogether different thing from surrendering one's autonomy.

This is what Antoine de Saint-Exupéry meant when he said: 'Love does not consist in gazing at each other, but looking outward together in the same direction.' Having said that, togetherness essentially means growing closer through shared experience, so we must be careful not to downplay the importance of doing things together, whether it is travelling, enjoying a joint hobby, playing with the children, or making love.

Getting through hard times with mutual help and support is also a crucial element; transcending difficulties together is one of the hallmarks of real love. Togetherness can also be engendered by embracing the 'otherness' of one's partner. For example, whilst we might have no interest in their career as such, we can be enthusiastic and supportive on their behalf.

We can also have separate hobbies and pastimes but still show interest in our partner's grand passion for stamp collecting, model car racing or whatever. However, when a hobby takes over someone's life and the other person feels shut out, such as the classic 'golf widow', that is pushing things too far.

Importance of shared goals

More important than anything we *do*, however, is what we think and believe. Research has shown that shared goals can be the single most important factor in keeping a relationship together. In practical terms this means our world views and our values, or, to put it another way, our overall outlook on life.

By 'overall outlook' I mean our attitude towards such things as relationships, both within families and between couples; the importance of friendships; spiritual matters such as a belief in God or otherwise; the need to be ambitious or the desire to just 'plod along'; and whether we have a 'glass half full' or 'glass half empty' view of life. It is not essential that our views on these matters are totally aligned, but there must be a meeting of minds at some level. This does not necessarily discount the possibility of 'agreeing to disagree' on some issues.

Perfection – a barrier to love

Perhaps the greatest barrier to love in today's world is the increasing pressure to achieve perfection in every area of our lives, as exemplified by the growing tendency to regard having plastic surgery, breast enhancements and botox injections as the 'norm'. However, it is not just our physical appearance that must be flawless; our sexual performance, our capability as parents, and just about every other human activity must also conform to a level of sustained excellence that is inhuman.

Because of this, people are increasingly going into relationships with the expectation – fuelled by pressures from society, advertisers, the media and themselves – that the person they commit to will be the personification of goodness, understanding, rampant sexuality, emotional sensitivity, and everything else a man or woman could want in a partner.

We need to let go of all such expectations because people are not robots; they are human and they have human flaws and weaknesses. It is only by accepting someone in the full range of their humanity that true intimacy and love can begin to grow.

In this context, it seems fitting to end with the passage from the New Testament book of *Corinthians* that is often quoted at weddings: 'Love is patient, love is kind … it is not self-seeking, it is not easily angered, it keeps no record of wrongs … It always protects, always trusts, always hopes, always perseveres.'

- Forget the idea of finding one person who will complete you.

- Being passionate about someone means more than having sex.

- Accepting someone with all their faults is the key to loving them.

Love needs the right conditions, principally time and nurture. It does not just happen and nor can it be forced.

Conclusions

Assumptions are the termites of relationships.
Henry Winkler

Helping the reader to gain insights into the complex assortment of psychological factors that come into play when two people decide to enter into a relationship has been the rationale for this book. If I were asked to single out a key theme, it perhaps would be the goal of dispelling the many myths, misconceptions, and assumptions that present themselves automatically whenever the word 'relationship' is mentioned.

I remember being greatly amused on hearing how a friend of one of my sons told a long-term girlfriend that he wanted to move on. Having agonized over the most sensitive but direct way of broaching the subject, he eventually settled for: 'We need to redefine the nature of our association.' To paraphrase those wonderfully prosaic words, perhaps we all need to *define* the nature of our associations before we commit ourselves to being with someone on an ongoing basis; in other words to decide exactly what it is *both* people expect to encounter and to deal with on the journey ahead, and how best to prepare for that.

If that sounds somewhat clinical and unromantic perhaps it is a small price to pay for attempting to 'get it right' and thus perhaps sparing yourself the agony, heartache and recrimination that come from a break-up. The principles examined in this book do not represent a guarantee against that happening in themselves; life – and relationships – are not like that. However, by at least taking some time to consider the bigger picture that has hopefully been flagged up by these psychological 'x factors', and learning to step back from the 'wow factor' that draws us in time and again, it is my hope that you will be better prepared to place your relationships on a stronger footing from the start.

Like everything else in life, relationships are a learning process; the more we can accept that we never stop finding out new things about why we are attracted to particular people, and why we behave in certain ways when that initial chemistry grows into something more, the greater chance there is that our relationships will survive the test of time. A good relationship should be like a fine wine – it should get better with age; it can be seen as a voyage of discovery that is enriching and sustaining, involving the development of mutual nurture, caring, and love, and the personal growth of both parties.

Learning is best when it comes from a wide variety of sources, and there are resources at the back of this book – publications about various aspects of relationships and love, as well as websites for organizations that offer advice and counselling in this field – to provide further insights, as well as help and support if it is needed. But, as useful as these things are, we must remember the words of Benjamin

Disraeli, who said: 'Experience is the child of Thought, and Thought is the child of Action. We cannot learn men from books.'

In the end, everything comes down to attitude, more specifically a willingness to listen, to understand, to be open and honest, and, within reason, to accept. It is about mastering the art of true connection and intimacy, which in turn is about satisfying a very human need to which we are all entitled to aspire: to have someone with whom you can share your dreams and schemes, your good days and your bad days, your fears, your tears, and the passing years; in essence someone to be there for you – and you for them.

I shall end with a delightful little extract from *Winnie-the-Pooh* by A. A. Milne that encapsulates this sentiment: 'Piglet sidled up to Pooh from behind. "Pooh!" he whispered. "Yes, Piglet?" "Nothing," said Piglet, taking Pooh's paw. "I just wanted to be sure of you."'

By putting at least some of the principles in these pages into practice, I sincerely hope that, in the right way, you can be increasingly sure of the person you choose to be with.

Resources

Books for further reading

Anatomy of Love by Helen Fisher (Ballantine, 1994).
A comprehensive history and analysis of mating, marriage, sexual attraction, and infidelity, by an acknowledged expert in her field.

Building a Love That Lasts by Charles D. Schmitz and Elizabeth A. Schmitz (Jossey Bass, 2008)
Two of America's best-known authorities on love and marriage reveal the secrets that enable couples to develop and sustain long-lasting relationships.

Families and How to Survive Them by Robin Skynner and John Cleese (Cedar, 1993)
A renowned bestseller focusing on the psychological factors operating behind the scenes in families and relationships, written jointly by a leading family therapist and the star of *Monty Python's Flying Circus* and *Fawlty Towers*.

Getting the Love You Want by Harville Hendrix (Pocket Books, 2005)
A perennial favourite suggesting ways for couples to achieve greater understanding of their relationships, and thus make them more loving, supporting and revitalized.

Magnetic Partners by Stephen J. Betchen (Free Press, 2010)
An examination of the role of conflict in relationships, including why couples fight about the same thing over and over again, and how attraction can be sparked by a shared 'master conflict'.

Rebuilding When Your Relationship Ends by Bruce Fisher and Robert Alberti (Impact, 2008)
One of the best known guides to surviving relationship breakdown and the difficulties of being single again, often used as a standard text book on divorce recovery courses.

The Art of Loving by Erich Fromm (Thorsons, 1995)
Regarded as a classic of its kind and written by a major figure in the world of psychoanalysis, this beautifully written, easy-to-read little book examines all aspects of love in many different settings.

The Dance of Intimacy by Harriet Lerner (Harper Perennial, 1990)
A woman's guide to making courageous acts of change in order to enhance intimacy and greater connectedness in relationships, as well as developing a deeper sense of self.

The Psychology of Romantic Love by Nathaniel Branden (Tarcher/Penguin, 2008)
Explores the nature of romantic love, intimacy and sexuality on many levels, and offers a new vision of love that is both realistic and sustainable in an 'anti-romantic' age.

The Road Less Travelled by M. Scott Peck (Arrow, 1990)
Perhaps the most famous popular psychology book of our time; an inspirational, insightful and revolutionary look at spiritual growth, love, relationships, traditional values, and life.

The Seven Principles for Making Marriage Work by John Gottman and Nan Silver (Orion, 2000)
A relationship guide based on the use of scientific procedures to observe the habits of married couples in detail over many years; contains practical questionnaires and exercises.

The Transformation of Intimacy by Anthony Giddens (Polity Press, 1993)
An examination of the sexual revolution, and an analysis of the role of sexuality, gender and identity in modern culture, written by a former professor of Sociology and fellow of King's College, Cambridge.

Who Moved My Cheese by Dr Spencer Johnson
(Vermilion, 1998)
An international bestseller that uses a simple parable about
four characters living in a maze to demonstrate how to deal
with change in the most beneficial and productive way.

Why We Love by Helen Fisher (Holt McDougal, 2005)
By the celebrated author of *Anatomy of Love*, this is an equally
compelling volume analysing the biological, chemical and
anthropological underpinnings for the phenomenon we know
as romantic love.

Why Women Have Sex by Cindy Meston and David Buss
(Vintage, 2010)
The title says it all about this detailed analysis of the many
reasons – 237 in all according to the psychologists who
wrote the book – behind the female sex drive.

Organizations offering advice and therapy

UK and Europe

British Association for Counselling and Psychotherapy –
www.bacp.co.uk

College of Sexual and Relationship Therapists –
www.cosrt.org.uk

Couples Counselling Network –
www.ukcouplescounselling.com

Institute of Family Therapy – www.ift.org.uk

Pink Therapy (for sexual and gender minorities) –
www.pinktherapy.com

Relate (relationship counselling) – www.relate.org.uk

Tavistock Centre for Couple Relationships –
www.tccr.org.uk

UK Council for Psychotherapy – www.psychotherapy.org.uk

American Psychological Association – www.apa.org

European Association for Psychotherapy –
www.europsyche.org

USA

National Register of Health Service Providers in Psychology – www.nationalregister.org

National Board for Certified Counselors – www.nbcc.org

Australia

Psychotherapy and Counselling Federation of Australia – www.pacfa.org.au

Index

abandonment 90
acceptance 148, 167, 191–2, 194–5
addictions 118
  everyday 39
  features of 36
  and repetition compulsion 129
addictive love 36
adrenaline 118
agape 185
Ainsworth, Mary 34
Allen, Woody 159, 161
aloneness 40, 41
ambivalent attachment 34
amphetamines 117–18
Anderson, Margaret 186
anima 25
animus 25
annihilation, threat of 38
anxieties, unthinkable 39
anxiety, psychological effects 47
arguments, and keeping relationship alive 96
Assagioli, Roberto 185
associations, nature of 197
attachment styles 34, 97, 138
  complementary 138

attachment theory 33–5
attention-seeking 74
attention span 69
  average 68
attitude 199
attraction
  conscious expectations 123
  'Facebook of' 130–1
  law(s) of 121
  public aspects 123
  sexual 122
  unconscious 123–7
attractiveness, reassurance of 177
authority figures 128
avoidant attachment 34

beliefs
  foundational 83–4, 105
  of how perceived by others 87
Betchen, Stephen 139
betrayal
  feeling of 178–9
  gender differences in responses to 50–1, 172–3
Bible 20

bipolar disorder 114
bonding 33–5, 129
Bowlby, John 34
Boy George 163
brain, structure change
       59–60
Branden, Dr Nathaniel
       149–50
breastfeeding 129
British Psychological Society
       116–17
British Social Attitudes
       Survey 171
Browning, Robert 1
Bullock, Sandra 19, 22
Buss, David 50, 175

career, changing 62
Casanova 166–7
CBT 87, 92
celebrities, idolization of 26
change
   as continuous for life
       59–60
   inevitability of 62
   negative perception of
       56–9
   as opportunity 65
   steps in dealing with 59
character
   building 101
   self-esteem and 85
'chemistry' 189

children, birth 62–3
Cleese, John 125, 127
co-dependency,
       characteristics 37–8
Cocker, Joe 111
cognitions, faulty 92
Cognitive Behavioural
       Therapy (CBT) 87, 92
commitment 96, 188, 190–1
   avoiding 152–3
communication 67–79
   in conflict handling
       105–6
   core conditions for 76–7
   and intimacy 148
   and love 188
   as maker or breaker 71–2
   need to be two-way 67
   non-verbal, decoding
       73–5
   point of no return 77–8
   sex as form of 166–8
   time and 72
   see also listening
'commuter marriages' 72
companionate love 190–1
completion of self 21, 22–3
compromise 105
conflict 95–107
   communication as crucial
       in handling 105–6
   gender differences in
       handling 99–101

maintenance behaviours
104–5
master 139, 142
as no-go area 100
perpetual 102–4
resolving constructively
101–2
styles differences 96–9
'twin-in' 140
confluent love 190–1
Confucius 65
congruence 76–7
connection
searching for 166
true 199
conscious mind 124
consummate love 190–1
contempt 103
control, paradox of 46–7
coping mechanisms 47
couple, becoming part of
144
courage 148–9
crimes of passion 47
criticism 103
cross-addiction 38
'cuddle hormone' 119

Daly, Helen 176
Daly, Jeff 67
Davis, Keith 142
defensiveness 103
denial 114–16, 141

Dicks, Henry 123–4
diet pills 118
Dillner, Dr Luisa 21
Disraeli, Benjamin 198–9
distance, keeping your 52–3
distortion 114–15
'divine accident' 145, 186,
189
divorce 156
adultery as grounds for
172
divorce recovery groups 40
doom, predictors of 103
'doormat' 12
dopamine 118
'dump first' scenario 153–5
Dyer, Dr Wayne 81

effort, putting in 2–3
ego boundaries, collapse of
31, 109
'elastic band syndrome'
151–2
emotional-physical split
172–3
emotions, giving vent to 100
empathy 76
empty love 191
endorphins 119
eros 185
'eye love' 129

family systems exercise 125–6

fantasizing 114, 179–80
  obsessive 110, 111
fatuous love 191
Faulkner, William 121
fear
  of intimacy 149, 151–5
  of loneliness 40–2
  as negative behaviour
    basis 55
  and reluctance to
    communicate 71, 106
fear-based relationships
  44–6
female sexuality 175–6
Fennell, Dr Melanie 85
field of availabilities 142
field of desirables 143
filter model of relationships
  142–3
Fisher, Bruce 41
Fisher, Dr Helen 72, 174,
  180
'fix me' demand 23–4
flowing process, life as 60–1
foundational beliefs 83–4,
  105
'The Four Horsemen of the
  Apocalypse' 103
Freud, Sigmund 32, 109,
  127–9, 160, 178–9
friendship 191–2
  passionate 191
Fromm, Erich 186, 189, 190

frustration 32
  sexual 89

gender myths 14–16
gentleness 104
Gibran, Kahlil 53
Giddens, Anthony 190–1
goals, shared 193–4
Gottman, John 102–3, 104
growth, as individuals 52

Hendrix, Harville 191
Henry, Lenny 9
Hepburn, Audrey 17
hidden agendas 102
Homer 111
honeymoon phase, emerging
  from 9–10
hopes, on entering
  relationship 143–4
humility 101–2
Hybels, Bill 149

identity, taking on new 144
idolization 26
Imperial College 117
infatuation 190–1
infidelity 49, 171–82
  gender differences
    regarding 172–3
  increased lifespans impact
    180–2
  low self-esteem and 177–8

'inner critic' 92
insecure attachment 138
insecurity 35
Institute of Family Therapy
    125
intimacy 147–58
    communication and 148
    as component of love
        190–1
    in conflict resolution 104
    definitions 147
    fear of 149, 151–5
    knowing yourself 156–7
    mastering the art of 199
    practical exercise in
        149–50
    routes to 155–6
    sex and 164

James, William 95, 100
jealousy
    at bonding between
        mother and baby 63
    as characteristic of human
        behaviour 49
    gender and 50–1
    healthy 46
    as individual response
        49–50
    as self-harm 47–9
job, changing 62
Johnson, Dr Spencer 59
Jung, Carl 25

Keats, John 13
Keen, Sam 183
Kerckhoff, Alan 142
Kinsey Report 175
'knowing without knowing'
    124
knowing yourself 156–7

Laumann, Dr Edward O. 169
learning process,
    relationships as 198
Lee, Bruce 186
Lerner, Dr Harriet 147–8,
    155–6
Levenson, Robert 103
libido 160
life, as flowing process 60–1
life-changing events,
    neglectful approach to
    10–11
life events, effects 61
'like attracts like' 139
liking 191
limerence 113–14
Lipton, Bruce 124–5
listening
    active 70
    art of 69
    developing skills of 69–71
    statistics about 68–9
'living in each other's
    pockets' 43
lodus 185

loneliness
    fear of 40–2
    ghost of 41
loss, experiences of 153
love 183–95
    addictive 36
    at first sight 28, 188–9
    categories of 184–6
    communication and 188
    companionate 190–1
    confluent 190–1
    consummate 190–1
    definitions of 184–9
    descriptions of 111, 195
    empty 191
    fatuous 191
    ideal of 13–14
    inner progressiveness of
        145, 186
    learning the art of 189–90
    needing 14
    perfection as barrier to
        194–5
    quotations about 186–7
    romantic 190–1
        studies of 116–17
    searching for 166, 167
    shared goals and 193–4
    togetherness element
        192–3
    triangular theory of
        190–1
love maps 122–3

magical thinking 36–7
maintenance behaviours
    104–5
mania 185
manic depression 114
marriage
    polygamous 180
    Western idea 180
master conflicts 139, 142
mate-guarding 49–50, 51,
    174–5
Maugham, W. Somerset 55,
    56
Mead, Margaret 7
meaning, shared 104
Meltzer, Brad 147
men, primary love needs 15
Meston, Cindy 175
Milne, A. A. 199
'mind reading', expectation
    of 73–4
'missing parts', search for
    24–5
monogamy 180
mother love, early, as
    template 129–30
murder 46–7
mutual undertaking 19

nature 84
needs
    driving relationships 7–8
    right to have 16–17

unmet 11–12
negative voices 92
negativity, spiral of 71–2
neuropeptides 119
Nolte, Dorothy Law 84–5
non-verbal communication,
    decoding 73–5
nurture 84
nymphomania 166–7

Obsessive Compulsive
    Disorder (OCD) 60,
    117, 118
obsessive fantasizing 110,
    111
OCD 60, 117, 118
Oedipus complex 178–9
'omnipotence' theory 32–3
openness to experiences
    51–2
'opposites attract' 24, 135–
    6, 139
orgasms 119, 161, 175
'other half' 20–2, 183
    ancient roots of myth 20
outlook, overall 193–4
oxytocin 119

paranoia 44
parents
    becoming 62–3
    opposite sex, and
        attraction 129–30

partner selection
    areas involved 123
    filter model of 142–3
Pascal, Blaise 31
passion 190–2
PEA 117–18
Peck, Scott 31, 122, 187
perfection, as barrier to love
    194–5
Perrett, David 130
phenylethylamine (PEA)
    117–18
Plato 20, 111
Player, Gary 3
point of no return 77–8
possessiveness 46, 174
pragma 185
pride 4
primary caregiver 33–5
projection 25–8, 89
Prozac 118
psychological compatibility
    143
psychological contact,
    making 77
psychological 'drivers' 119
psychosexual stages 160
psychosynthesis 185

reaction formation 141
reality principle 32
relationship addiction 36–7
repetition compulsion 128–9

resentment 71, 95
reward-based behaviour 118
Rilke, Rainer Maria 52–3
Rogers, Carl 60–1, 76–7
romantic love 190–1
    studies of 116–17
Roosevelt, Eleanor 93
Roosevelt, Franklin D 41

Saint-Exupéry, Antoine de
    43, 192
Sartre, Jean-Paul 43
Schmitz, Charles 162
Schmitz, Elizabeth 162
Schwarz, Jeffrey 60
secondary caregiver 35
secure attachment 34, 97,
    138
self-acceptance, working
    towards 91–2
self-deception 115
self-esteem 81–93
    and character 85
    fluidity 83
    low
        and fear of intimacy
            151–2
        and infidelity 177–8
        model of 85–6
        roots of 92
        therapy for 91–2
        vicious circle of 87–91
    maintaining 87, 88

self-fulfilling prophecies 90,
    91, 138, 152, 177
self-harm, jealousy as 47–9
separateness 52–3
serotonin 118
sex 159–70
    casual 169–70, 176
    as form of communication
        166–8
    gender differences in
        approaches to 169–70
    and intimacy 164
    mental factor in 164
    as not crucial factor
        162–3
    as pressure 165–6
    talking about 165–6
    unrealistic expectations
        160–2
'sex life' 159
sexuality
    female 175–6
    variations in 63–4
Shakespeare, William 171
shared meaning system 104
Shaw, George Bernard 47
Skynner, Robin 125, 127,
    140
'smother mother' type 153
soul mate 20–1, 99
stagnation 52, 65
Sternberg, Robert 190–1
'stiff upper lip' 100

Stone, Sharon 16
stonewalling 103
storge 185
suppression of feelings 71, 95

Tavistock Clinic 123
Tennov, Dorothy 113–14
Thurber, James 5
Tillich, Paul 187
time
    and communication 72
    effect of 16–17
togetherness 192–3
Tolstoy, Leo 184
transcendence 166
transference 12–13, 27,
    127–8
transparency, mutual 147
triangular theory of love
    190–1
Twain, Mark, 187
'twin-in-conflict' 140

unconditional positive regard
    (UPR) 76, 77

unconscious mind, power of
    124–5

'Velcro phase' 9
vicarious living 24, 136
virginity 167
vulnerability 5, 148

'wallflowers' 127
Walpole, Sir Hugh 145,
    185–6, 189
Walsch, Neale Donald 29
Warnes, Jennifer 111
Wilde, Oscar 135
Willow Creek Association
    149
Winfrey, Oprah 82
Winkler, Henry 197
Winnicott, Donald 38–9, 40
withholding 149
women, primary love needs
    15

Zeus 20